Yoga Nine Ways

Awakening to Source with the Enneagram & Yoga

By Debi Saraswati Lewis

Founder of Joyflow Yoga

Yoga Nine Ways
Awakening to Source with the Enneagram & Yoga

CreateSpace

Yoga / Enneagram / Self-help / Psychology / Emotional IQ / Spirituality

First Edition (July, 2012)
First Printing (July, 2012)
Second Printing (November, 2015)

ISBN-10: 1511943920

ISBN-13: 9781511943925

When we are in the world of the thinking mind,
we are somewhere in the remembered past or the imagined future.
We are in a world of thought, memory, concept,
idea, opinion and belief.

We are not here now.
What we are experiencing is not truth
and reality of the present moment.

In a very real sense, the past is intruding into our experience
of the present moment, coloring and distorting it.
All those limiting beliefs and painful experiences of the past
adversely affect our experience of life.

To awaken simply means to awaken out of the world
of the thinking mind into the world of the present moment.
This does not mean that your memory of the past
or your sense of the future disappears.

You still participate within the world of time, but you are no longer
identified with or defined by those memories from the past
or imaginings into the future.

You come to know yourself as the One who exists in this moment.
You know that only the present moment can fulfill you and so you
choose to live more and more fully in the present moment.
The present moment becomes the very foundation of your life.

As you awaken, your experience of yourself
and the world will dramatically change.
Fear, anxiety and conflict disappear
as you enter into a world of
love, peace and abundance.

You come to know yourself as LOVE.
You encounter the living Presence of God
within you and within everything around you.
Separation dissolves as you enter into Oneness.

This is what is meant by enlightenment. It is what Buddha spoke of.
It is what Jesus spoke of. It is what Lao-Tzu and Krishna spoke of.
It is what God promised to Abraham.

The Daily Guru – www.portalstopeace.com – Tutte Peever

Acknowledgements

This book has been a long time in the making and many people, friends, family and students, have been supportive and encouraging to me along the way. First I want to thank my parents for introducing me to the Enneagram. They fostered my search for meaning in my life and love of learning.

Then I had the good fortune to meet the inspiring and spunky Tina Thomas, who, unlike me, does things much faster and is now Dr. T of all things wise and wonderful. Tina inspired me to take the Enneagram Institute certification training.

Special thanks to my Enneagram teachers Don Riso and Russ Hudson for their knowledge, inspiration and especially their patience with me as I took probably the longest time on record to finish my certification with them. Almost all of the Enneagram information in this book is from their teaching.

My first yoga teacher Janie Strickland opened my eyes to the healing power of yoga. Many teachers along the way, primarily Eric Schiffman, Beryle Bender Birch and Rod Stryker, have been instrumental in building my understanding and teaching of yoga. My many dear students over the years have given me the gift of their time, love and feedback, enabling me to find my heart's calling to become a yoga teacher.

So many people have read and encouraged this book along the way and I know I won't be able to remember them all, but big thanks to Jean Smith, Virginia Earnest, John Cartwright, Deirdre Danahar, Laura Moore, my mom Dorothy Porter and my final editor, Rachel Ferrell. Special thanks to Cindy Clark for helping me put in finishing touches, layout and cover art.

Thanks to my husband, Kevin, for putting up with my crazy passion for yoga, the Enneagram, and all things impractical and esoteric. And of course, last but certainly not least, none of this would have happened without the persistence and love of The Beloved that meets me in my heart every time I call, and for Divine Guidance, that continues to appear in both physical and non-physical forms, to remind me to believe in myself.

Notes from the Author

• All names and some details have been changed in the personal illustrations to protect confidentiality.

• This book is about how to use yoga and the Enneagram together. To learn more about the Enneagram, I recommend any of the Riso-Hudson books. A list of their books is in the reference section at the end of this book. The section on the Enneagram is a summary of their teaching and I hope it will encourage you to investigate further.

Likewise, if you are unfamiliar with yoga or any of the yogic techniques referred to in this book, I recommend finding a competent teacher. This book is not meant to teach yoga.

• As when participating in any physical exercise or spiritual practice, please do not neglect to seek advice from the appropriate physician or therapist as needed.

Contents

Introduction

"Withdrawn types (Fours, Fives, and Nines) need to engage the body. **Compliant types** (Ones, Twos, and Sixes) need to quiet the mind. **Assertive types** (Threes, Sevens, and Eights) need to open the heart."[1]

Which one are you?

There are three centers of intelligence within each of us. The brain, of course, is an obvious center of intelligence. Yet research is now showing scientific evidence that we also have intelligence in the heart and, in fact, throughout the whole body. Head, Heart and Gut. This book is based on the idea, realized by Don Riso and Russ Hudson, leading developers of the Enneagram, that we have a tendency to be more oriented toward one of these intelligences and to neglect one of them. The one in the middle gets tangled, or confused, with the dominant intelligence center. For example, we might go into a situation with the Heart Center leading. Then the Gut intelligence engages, resulting in rushing emotionally into a situation with a confused mental awareness. The Head Center is left behind.[2]

When the Body (or Gut), Heart and Head intelligences are balanced and healthy, we will be physically grounded, open-hearted and clear minded.

What does it mean to be physically grounded or healthy in Gut intelligence? When you are physically grounded and aware of your body's intelligence you will have healthy boundaries, a sense of presence and focus, a tendency to live in the present moment and to move with confidence. You will feel "at home" in your body, solid and stable. And when you are not grounded physically, you will not feel connected to the present moment and will find it difficult to respond easily to life's changes. You may also feel clumsy and be accident-prone.

What does it mean to be open-hearted or healthy in Heart intelligence? You will have a healthy awareness of your emotions and the emotions of others, as well as the ability to acknowledge and release emotions wisely. You will feel authentic and true in your heart and have a strong intuition. When not heart healthy, your emotions may pull you around like a leaf in the wind or you may feel them suppressed by a heavy coat of armor.

What does it mean to be clear-minded or healthy in Head intelligence? I refer here not to your actual degree of smartness or education, rather to your ability to cultivate a quiet mind. Can you let go of the anxious busy-mind and find a place of inner guidance within yourself. The anxious, cluttered "monkey mind" leads to doubts, fears, insecurity and exhaustion. Quiet mind allows you to experience yourself at a whole new level, your True Self, beyond busy mind and limited body.

This is a book about how to use the wisdom of both yoga and the Enneagram to find balance in these three centers of intelligence: Gut, Heart and Head. When we are healthy and balanced we can be more aware of our essential spiritual nature and connection to Source. Therefore, this is also a book about how to use yoga and the Enneagram to become more aware, more awake, more in touch with spirit. It's about realizing what patterns of consciousness get in the way of our experience of the Divine. What gets in the way of our happiness? If we are truly made in the image of God why don't we feel like we are? We have all had great moments of connection, wonderful spiritual high points of awareness, only to find that given the least annoying life circumstance, we revert to old patterns that are less than glorious.

A friend of mine came home one evening, after participating in a wonderful evening of meditation, to find her front door open, her dog roaming the neighborhood and her child and babysitter missing. All ended well, but you can bet she lost her just-tuned-up spiritual cool! If we could only just spend our lives meditating in some blissful place in some mystical mountain cave with a Master teacher, wouldn't we all be enlightened by now? So, I want to encourage us all that we are attempting the highest spiritual practice when we try to be spiritually conscious in the midst of our chaotic lives, minute by minute, hour by hour, day by day.

Awakening

What does awakening mean? It certainly means more than just not being asleep. When Gautama, the Buddha, was asked whether he was a teacher, a prophet, a guru, or what, He simply replied, "I am awake." Awakening means to be aware on a different level than the obvious physical one we're accustomed to living in. Awakening is to be perceptive to a deeper reality of energy. Awakening is being aware of your True Self, Sat Nam, I am That. The phrase "being present" means much more than simply being here in the usual sense. It means being totally present to the moment, not reliving the past or worrying about the future. Ram Das put that phrase on our culture's radar with the '60's classic *Be Here Now*.[3] In the next few chapters we will go into the nature of reality, of consciousness, of Spirit, and flesh out (pun intended) the idea of awakening as we explore the essence of Yoga and of the Enneagram.

Source

The word Source is a great word that expresses what cannot be expressed in words. Many times our words for the Divine are limiting and can create conflicts. Cultural misunderstandings, and even wars, have taken place because of our disagreements over what we experience as Source, God, Mother/Father, Great Spirit, Allah, Brahma, Jehovah, The Force, The Tao, The Divine, etc. Throughout history, we have called this experience of Source by many names. The problem comes when we misunderstand the words, concepts, beliefs and cultural habits for the real experience.[4]

There is a well-known story that illustrates this. A group of blind men encounter an elephant in the forest. Each of them experiences a different part of the elephant. One finds the trunk and describes it as a snake or a hose; another compares the elephant's leg to a strong column in the temple and yet another finds the tail and thinks it is a rope, and so on. They all begin to argue as to the nature of the elephant, not realizing that each of them is simply experiencing a part of the whole elephant. Religion is just like the elephant; it represents only a part of the possible experience of the whole. However, a spiritual experience is different in that it has not (yet) been categorized and limited by words and beliefs about it.

The Great Teachers have all had that real experience of Source and tried to take us there. The experience of Source is an overwhelming sense of coming Home, of Joy, Peace, Power and most of all Love. We say "God is Love" and don't even fully realize what that means. WHAT IF we are made of God-stuff and we are Love? What if we could live life with this awareness? There is really no way to fully express in words this experience of Source; it must simply be experienced. I can only say that once you have had the experience, nothing can ever take it away. It is a knowing deep in your soul.

This book is about how we can live life connected and awakened to Source. Both the wisdom of yoga and of the Enneagram are time-tested tools that will help us identify both that which interferes with awakening to Source and what that awakening looks and feels like. I'd like to give you a few suggestions about how to read this book. Although I hope you eventually read it all, you might like to start in the middle. If you are very familiar with yoga and energetic anatomy, start right in with the Enneagram. If you are already familiar with the Enneagram, explore the sections on yoga first, and then skip on over to the yoga recommendations. If you are already familiar with both, go right on to the recommendations; enjoy and then go back to read the rest if you like.

What is Yoga?

"You cannot do yoga. Yoga is your natural state.
What you can do are yoga exercises, which may reveal
to you where you are resisting your natural state."

– Sharon Gannon, Jivamukti Yoga

In this country yoga has become well known as a really great exercise and, in a sense it has been diluted and reduced to simply a good workout. As we go into Energetic Anatomy you'll get a sense of why yoga is such a profound exercise, since it involves every aspect of our being. But the Yoga Sutra defines yoga as the state in which one no longer identifies with the fluctuations of the mind and instead reflects deeper within to a place beyond ordinary perception. When this happens one discovers one's true nature, which is beyond the ego and beyond the physical and even the mental ways of experiencing life.[5] So although there is a physical component to a yoga practice, yoga actually has more to do with your mind, heart and soul. It's really not about whether you can touch your toes or do a headstand for five minutes.

That said, there are many ways to do the physical practice of yoga. We now have specific styles of yoga that seem very different from each other. Originally, yoga was taught individually from Guru to student, and was customized for each student's personal needs and abilities. Now yoga is generally taught in group classes, and not all kinds of yoga are helpful for all students. This vast variety, combined with the minimizing, or actual elimination, of the deeper practices of yoga such as meditation and pranayama (the study of the breath), has led to a lot of confusion about yoga.

Three quite distinct styles of yoga have shaped the practice of yoga in the West. They all originated from one Indian Guru, **Krishnamacharya**, who taught, among many, three students who needed different approaches and who all later came to the West and developed distinct styles of yoga. **B.K.S. Iyengar** emphasized correct alignment and precision in each posture as it is held. Props are used to enable anyone to find the correct form within their individual abilities. Postures are held quite a long time and often several times with different modifications. Thus, it is called **Iyengar Yoga** and has a very therapeutic focus.[6]

Pattabhi Jois emphasized creating heat, energy and strength by the continuous flow of movements and a particular breathing technique, the Ujjayi breath. This is known as **Ashtanga Yoga** and is very strenuous, best suited to young athletic students. This practice is very powerful, rewarding and fun; it increases energy and flexibility like nothing else.[7] The Ashtanga style led to the creation of a form of yoga called **Power Yoga** or **Vinyasa**, which means flow, or placed in sequence, that is more variable and adaptable to individual needs. There are now many Vinyasa teachers with different individual styles; Eric Schiffman is one of my favorite teachers.[8]

T.K.V. Desikachar, the son of Krishnamacharya, felt that yoga must be individualized to serve the student and his particular needs. He preferred to work with students one-on-one and his ability to heal with yoga was his primary legacy. This yoga is now known as **Viniyoga** and it is now often taught in group settings. It has a strong emphasis on bringing breath and movement together dynamically.[9] Each of these methods has influenced not only my training but also most of the yoga practiced in the West today. I mention this because as you explore the world of yoga, the form it takes needs to be a good fit for you, your personality and your physical needs. Some styles of yoga may actually increase your negative tendencies if you are not aware of it. I will go into this more in the specific recommendations later on.

Energetic Anatomy

"We are not physical beings having a spiritual experience. Rather, we are spiritual beings having a physical experience."

– Teilhard de Chardin

We generally perceive of ourselves as physical beings. How do you identify yourself? Are you tall or short, overweight or thin, blonde or brunette, etc...? What are your roles or job titles, even your personality traits? But that is not you; it is about you. It is your packaging.

To take you out of the habit of physical thinking so you can perceive things from an energetic viewpoint, I'd like to give you some images. Science tells us that if we look at the physical scale of the molecules in your body, the actual space between those particles of matter is comparable to the spaces between stars in the universe. We seem solid but are mostly made of empty space.

The second image is to go very small to the size of an atom. When the atom is split, all that is left is energy. Everything in the universe including you is made of energy. This is what mystics and spiritual teachers have always claimed and science confirms it as well. The study of quantum physics even suggests that physical reality is influenced by consciousness.

Or consider the new research on water. *In The Hidden Messages in Water* Masaru Emoto illustrates that water has the ability to change its crystalline shape in response to thought.[10] You can hold a glass of water and concentrate on a quality and see in a microscope how the water changes. Our bodies are made of over 75% water, so what does that mean for us?

When Jesus, and other Awakened Masters, performed miracles, it seems miraculous to us looking at it from a physical perspective, but they saw reality on a subatomic energetic level and understood how to work with it. Jesus said we would do what he did and more. I think it's important to consider that they not only understood how to manipulate matter, but they also did the disciplined spiritual work to make their own bodies and minds vibrate at a high enough level to handle such transformations. The principles in this book I believe are tools to help you develop this spiritual discipline and insight.

The ancient yogis understood and mapped the energetic body and saw the relationship of the energetic body to the physical body. Some people are able to see the energetic body, also called the auric field. Its existence is now being confirmed through science, notably in physics and kerilian photography.[11] The aura is the energy containing and surrounding a living being. If you are healthy and happy, your aura will be strong and vibrant. Most of us can feel the aura.

Have you noticed the vibration when you walk into a room where someone is very excited or very angry? As we get more in touch with our energetic body, we reframe our experience of ourselves and thus our whole self-identity. Then we will experience life in a whole new way.

Energetic Anatomy is an Eastern science that is increasingly being recognized as valid by Western medicine. There are seven primary centers of energy called the **Chakras**. These vortexes of bio-electrical energy occur in the body in basically the same location as the physical nerve complexes and each corresponds to a certain aspect of life. Each center has its own dynamics of consciousness and each has a role to play in our lives. There are two channels of energy, the **ida** and the **pingala**, that flow through the body, crossing at each chakra. A central cord of energy that overlaps the physical spinal cord, is called the **sushumna**. When we are stressed, blocks are created in these energy channels. When we remove the energetic blocks, it increases the energy flow and all of the chakras become healthier, a rise of energy that results is called **kundalini**. Our medical symbol, the **caduceus** is actually an ancient diagram of this energetic pattern of healing.

The Seven Chakras

Crown – Spiritual – White/Lavender
3rd Eye – Perception – Purple/Indigo
Throat – Expression – Blue/Aqua
Heart – Love – Green
Solar Plexus – Power – Yellow
Sacral – Sex – Orange
Root – Survival – Red

This information about chakras is from Carolyn Myss's work.[12] She is a western-trained medical intuitive and has presented the chakras in a way that is easy to understand. She teaches the relationship between physical ailments and imbalances in the chakras.

The first chakra, the root chakra, is at base of spine. It is thought to be red, or contain the energy of **Red**. It concerns our place in the world, security and safety, fulfilling societal roles, ability to provide for life's necessities, ability to stand up for one-self and feeling "at home." The root chakra is our energetic seat of basic strength, power and life-force. When it is healthy, we feel grounded and strong.

The second chakra has the energy of **Orange** and is located in the genital region. It takes the strength from the root chakra and manifests it into the world as physical power. Its influence is reflected in our actions and creations (including pro-creation). The second chakra is concerned with blame and guilt, money and sex, power and control, creativity, ethics and honor in relationships.

The third chakra is **Yellow** and is found in the solar plexus, just below the breast bone. This chakra represents awareness and development of Self. It is concerned with trust, fear and intimidation, self-esteem, self-confidence, self-respect, care of others, responsibility for making decisions, sensitivity to criticism, and personal honor. It also signifies intellectual energy.

The fourth energy center, the heart chakra is **Green** energy and is the seat of Unconditional Love. It concerns the giving and receiving of love, as well as hatred, resentment and bitterness, grief, self-centeredness, loneliness and commitment, forgiveness and compassion, hope and trust. Our heart organ looks like our symbol of love and it's interesting to note that heart transplant recipients often report having new emotional experiences.

The fifth chakra is thought to be **Blue or Aqua** and is located in the throat. It is the chakra of making your will manifest, of speaking your truth. It concerns personal integrity and consistent speech, choice and strength of will, personal expression, following one's dream, using personal power to create, addiction, judgment and criticism, faith and knowledge, and the capacity to make decisions.

The sixth chakra is **Purple or Indigo** resides in the forehead and is associated with the mind. It has the most well known name, the Ajna center, and has been given the most importance among many spiritual seekers. Yet, I believe that all of the chakras are equally important and that emphasizing only one of them is a dangerous practice. The Ajna chakra is concerned with developing wisdom and intuition, self-evaluation, truth, intellectual abilities, feelings of adequacy, openness to ideas of others, ability to learn from experiences, emotional intelligence.

The seventh chakra is seen as **Lavender, White or all colors** and represents Oneness. It is located at the crown of head and is called the crown chakra. It is concerned with the union of the physical and the spiritual. It is the integration of all of the other chakras, and acts as sort of a transformer for them creating the experience of Source, a sense of Peace and Joy. The crown chakra also affects the ability to trust life, values, ethics, courage, humanitarianism, selflessness, ability to see larger patterns, faith and inspiration, spirituality and devotion.

The physical body is affected by the energetic body. For example, if the first chakra is weak the physical body will not feel grounded and physical problems may arise in the lower pelvis and legs. If the third chakra is weak or stressed, a person may have digestive issues. When my sister discovered she had a thyroid tumor, fifth chakra energy, she chose to get rid of it using unconventional natural therapies. As she found her own voice and a strong fifth chakra, she became healed on all levels of mind, body and spirit. Her whole life, including relationships, changed. This experience has strengthened her to become a confident, enthusiastic and inspiring healer.

How Yoga Affects the Chakras

What makes the practice of yoga such a healing exercise is that since we are energetic beings, each type of posture has a certain energetic effect on us. We can use this knowledge to choose what and how to practice. Back bending and chest opening postures will often release suppressed emotion and increase confidence because they primarily affect the third and fourth chakras. Standing postures are grounding because they strengthen and bring awareness to the first chakra which has to do with identity and security. Forward bending postures often deal with inflexible thinking, surrendering and relaxing. Balancing postures help to steady the mind and emotions. With inversions you may face fears, gain confidence and experience a different point of view. Parts of the body, both physical and energetic, are either experiencing a massage-like compression or are experiencing a stretching and opening, thus releasing tension and unblocking stagnant energy.

 Camel or Ustrasana

Let's take just one posture and look at its details. For example, Ustrasana, or Camel pose. The grounded base of Camel is the knees and shins; the fronts of the thighs and are stretching and held strong. These points are grounding and thus affect the first and second chakras. The solar plexus and chest are getting the most action and stretch so the third and fourth chakras are getting a huge release. Then when you take your head back, the throat chakra is opened up. No wonder Camel pose is a strong pose, often bringing up nausea and resistance, but also profound healing and insights.

As you will see, although types of postures have certain energetic effects in common, when you look at one certain posture you'll see that most, if not all, chakras are affected.

You can also do the posture in ways that emphasize certain chakras and bring your attention to certain chakras while in a posture. For example in Camel pose you could focus on the grounding strong action of the legs and abdomen or on the lift through your heart. While both are important, your focus will change the posture energetically.

Here's an example of how one pose, Virabhadrasana I, Warrior, can be done with three different intentions of focus: Gut, Heart and Head.

Warrior I or
Virabhadrasana I

1. **Warrior I – Grounded Body:** bring your focus to the strength in your legs, pressing down evenly through the four corners of each foot. Hug the leg muscles to the bones, the feet pulling toward each other isometrically and rotating the pelvis forward. Drop into your lunge deeper. As you breathe deeply, be aware of the strength and compression of your core muscles as you exhale and the expansion of the chest as you inhale. Reach up strongly with the arms. Take your gaze higher and notice how you have to bring your attention to your feet in order to balance.

2. **Warrior I – Open Heart:** From your foundation, lean forward and expand the heart. Reach up with the arms, taking them as far back behind you as you can. Keep puffing the heart open on each inhale. Imagine your body wrapped around a giant cosmic beach ball. A variation might be to take the arms out to the sides and look up. Feel your strength and your heart, taking in a big breath of gratitude.

3. **Warrior I – Calm Mind:** become steady in your foundation and your breath. Keep your gaze fixed on a point in front of you and relax your face. Can you stay in a deep lunge and become present to the fluctuations of breath and thought? Where does your mind go? Can you stay for a whole minute?

You can use this information in two ways. **You can design your whole practice to reflect your focus.** For example, if you know you need a grounding practice you'll include a lot of poses that are grounding. **Or you can start your practice with an emphasis on your most Unused Center:** Gut, Heart or Head. The Enneagram shows us patterns in the way we use our centers. All of this is the basis for the rest of this book as we explore how to take wisdom from the Enneagram and combine it with the energetic anatomy of Yoga. I will be referring to different ways to do yoga and different ways to emphasize the chakras, or centers of the body, for each personality type.

What is the Enneagram?

For now we see only a reflection as in a mirror;
then we shall see face to face. Now I know in part; then I
shall know fully, even as I am fully known.

– 1 Corinthians 13:12, NIV

Yogic wisdom teaches us that our repetitive habits of thought become ingrained in us, much like waves in the ocean create sandbars and reshape the land. These ingrained patterns are called **"samscaras"** in the Sanscrit language (the traditional language of yoga) and they shape our personality.[13] I like this word samscara because it sounds like its meaning: it's the same ole, same ole, repetitious mind patterns that we focus on that create our internal scars and prevent us from experiencing the truth of our spirit and connection to Source.

The Enneagram is a beautiful model of these samscaras and how they operate within us. Our egos develop coping skills to deal with our needs, fears, beliefs and motivations. When we recognize these patterns within us we gain insight and clarity. We begin to understand ourselves and others with compassion. When we become aware of our unconscious patterns, we have a moment of choice and are no longer bound to negative reactions.

Ennea means **nine** in Greek. There are nine main personality types, though there are variations of each type. There are also certain relationships between the types as indicated by the lines of the Enneagram symbol. No type is better or more evolved than another, though each type does have levels of health. These are a range of identifying qualities and particular levels of functioning that indicate how self-aware and emotionally healthy a person is. We have all of the Enneagram personality patterns within us, yet one of them is our unconscious "default mode." Each type has its Spiritual Gifts, just as each type has its Spiritual Challenges for growth. It is important, and takes a bit of courage, to look at our ego-pattern honestly, both the uncomfortable negative part we prefer to avoid, but also to acknowledge our Spiritual Gifts.

The Enneagram symbol was originally brought to the West by George Ivanovich Gurdjieff in the late 1800's, from the mystery schools of the Middle East. He used the symbol and its geometric and spiritual principles in his teaching. Its present form as a psychological tool is due to the more contemporary inspiration of several psychologists and philosophers, including Oscar Ichazo from Argentina in the 1950's and then Claudio Naranjo in the 1970's at the Eselan Institute in Berkeley, California. The Enneagram also has roots in the concepts of the "Seven Deadly Sins" of the church. It has been taught through the Franciscan and Jesuit Orders, the Episcopal and Catholic Churches. It also has been compared to the Tree of Life of the Kabbalah in Jewish mysticism. Despite its relatively recent origin, the Enneagram of personality has become trusted worldwide as an amazingly accurate diagram of the structure of ego.[14]

The Enneagram has been developed by many teachers over the years. The main teachers with whom I have studied and whose Enneagram teachings I write about in this book are Don Riso and Russ Hudson. This book is informed and inspired by their teaching. Please see the Resources section for a list of their books and peruse their website for more information including personality tests and training. The next section is a brief description of how the pattern of the Enneagram works and a brief description of each personality type. I would like to thank Don Riso and Russ Hudson for allowing me to summarize their teaching.

How do you figure out which is your type? It is very important to look at the whole pattern of energy and attributes and not just latch on to a few qualities. For example, just because you are creative doesn't necessarily mean you are a Four, the Individualist. Just because you read a lot doesn't mean you are a Five, the Thinker. Just because you care about others doesn't mean you are a Two, the Helper or a Six, the Loyalist. Riso and Hudson's book *Discovering Your Personality Type* has an excellent independently tested and approved questionnaire which will help you identify your type.[15] You can also go to their website, **www.enneagraminstitute.com** and take the questionnaire online.

Seeing and understanding how your Enneagram pattern plays out in your life usually involves some deep and honest spiritual self-inquiry and soul searching. Once you realize your patterns you are likely to feel a bit uncomfortable, perhaps even experiencing the "dark night of the soul" explored by a contemporary spiritual teacher, Thomas Moore.[16] But if you move through it courageously you will come out on the other side, whole, at peace and connected to Source. You will experience that your Enneagram type is not defining you, but it shows the patterns of mind, the samscaras, that keep you from your Highest Self connected to Source.

Introduction End Notes:

1. *Understanding the Enneagram*, pg.277 by Don Riso and Russ Hudson. The practical guide to personality types, how to use it in daily life and in many settings. Has a section on comparisons, helpful if you can't decide your type. Also has the section that influenced this book about balancing the Centers.

2. *Understanding the Enneagram*, Ch. 7. The Centers, pg. 251, discusses the scrambling of the centers and their recommendation to work with the Unused Center.

3. *Be Here Now* by Ram Dass. The classic 60's introduction to yoga.

4. *The Message that Comes from Everywhere* by Gary L. Beckwith. Exploring the common core of the world's religions and modern science.

5. *How to Know God: The Yoga Aphorisms of Patanjali* by Swami Prabhavananda and Christopher Isherwood. My favorite editorial of the Yoga Sutras.

6. *Light on Yoga*, by B.K.S. Iyengar. The Iyengar classic, known as the "bible of modern yoga."

7. *Ashtanga: the Practice Manual* by David Swenson. A beautifully illustrated explanation of Ashtanga Yoga, the granddaddy of and inspiration for Vinyasa Yoga.

8. *Yoga: The Spirit and Practice of Moving into Stillness* by Erich Schiffman. An easy and inspiring read. Lovingly explains the spiritual practice of yoga.

9. *The Heart of Yoga: Developing a Personal Practice* by T.K.V. Desikachar. An in-depth study of moving with the breath, as well as the philosophical foundation of yoga.

10. *The Hidden Messages in Water* by Masaru Emoto and David A. Thayne.

11. *Hands of Light* by Barbara Ann Brennan A guide to healing through the human energy field.

12. *Energy Anatomy – The Science of Personal Power, Spirituality and Health* by Carolyn Myss, Ph.D., A guide to the chakras and energy healing.

13. *How to Know God. The Yoga Sutras.*

14. *Wisdom of the Enneagram*, pg. 20, by Don Richard Riso and Russ Hudson. Guide to Psychological and Spiritual Growth for the nine personality types.

15. *Discovering your Personality Type* by Don Riso and Russ Hudson. An essential introduction to the Enneagram which features the questionnaire.

16. *Dark Nights of the Soul* by Thomas Moore.

Patterns of the Enneagram

Passions, Fears and Desires

Each Enneagram type is driven by a particular Passion, Fear and Desire.[17] Realizing your own particular pattern requires a bit of uncomfortable self-inquiry, yet this is what elevates the Enneagram from a simple personality test to a spiritual journey. It goes way beyond whether or not you are introverted or extroverted and points to why you are. Because the Enneagram goes to such a deep intimate level of innocence and pain, it is important to approach ourselves with compassion and respect, being careful to not reduce it to a labeling game. The Enneagram really shows us the labels that we already have limiting us. As I outline each type, see if you notice these tendencies within yourself. Remember that we really have all of them, but one of them will be particularly strong in you.

Enneagram Wings

The pattern types on either side of a person's primary type pattern are called Wings. There are several variations of Enneagram philosophies concerning the Wings. Some teach that both wings on either side are like bird wings and are both brought into play in certain situations. Don Riso and Russ Hudson teach that we tend to favor one wing and that makes the most sense to me.[18] In geometry a circle has an infinite number of points, just as there are an infinite number of unique human beings. It makes sense that each of us will register on a point in this circle. A person might have textbook characteristics of one Enneagram point or they may be some balance of two points. For example, an Enneagram 4-wing-3 is quite different from a 4-wing-5, having a different set of variables. This creates many more patterns within the main nine types, which accounts for the vast variety of humanity. We are each individuals, not fully defined by a static pattern, but the pattern does give us valuable information.

Lines of Integration and Stress

The geometry of the Enneagram is beautiful in its intricacy. While we do stay the same basic type throughout our lives, we move horizontally, vertically and around the diagram diagonally as we evolve. Understanding how these diagonal lines work will help you identify your type. These patterns are also the foundation for how a yoga practice can be applied for each type, as you will see. The evolution of personality follows a logical and universal path. When a character in a story or movie does not follow this pattern, we instinctively know it and it feels false.

As you look at the structure of the Enneagram you will see two patterns of lines linking the types. Types Three, Six and Nine are linked in a triangular structure and the movement toward health is clockwise and toward stress is counterclock-wise. For example, when the anxious Type Six learns to relax into his gift of courage, he will begin to exhibit the peaceful harmony of a Nine, yet he won't actually become a Nine. Likewise, a normally peaceful Nine, when stressed, will not only experience the numbing, passive-aggressive aspects of her own type, but will also experience the anxiety of Six as the personality pattern flows along the lines. Yes, this will all make more sense as you read on. The other types are linked by a longer set of lines which move in the opposite direction, clockwise toward stress and counterclockwise toward health. Don Riso and Russ Hudson show how this structure plays out with each type as I summarize below.[19]

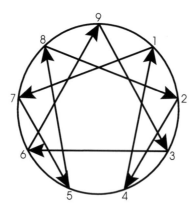

When we are stressed we move against the direction of arrows.

Moving counter clockwise: Anxious 6 becomes a workaholic like 3

Passive 9 becomes anxious like 6

Hardworking 3 becomes passive like 9

Moving clockwise: Uptight 1 becomes depressed like 4

Depressed 4 becomes co-dependent like 2

Co-dependent 2 becomes angry like 8

Angry 8 becomes cynical like 5

Cynical 5 becomes scattered like 7

Scattered 7 becomes critical like 1

When emotionally healthy and integrated, we move with the arrows.

Moving clockwise: Easy-going 9 begins to excel like 3

Excelling 3 plays well with others like 6

Organized 6 relaxes like easy-going 9

Moving counter clockwise: Focused 1 lightens up like 7

Playful 7 goes deep like 5

Deep 5 takes a stand like 8

Strong 8 finds their heart at 2

Loving 2 finds inner muse like 4

Creative 4 gets focused like 1

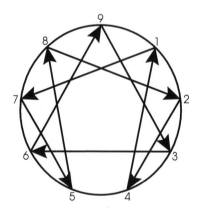

Levels of Development

We have now gone diagonally through the circle and around the circumference of the circle. One of Riso-Hudson's many contributions to the Enneagram is the Levels of Development, developed by Don Riso in 1977.[20] This takes us vertically up and down within the type with nine distinct categories of health and self-awareness. At the highest level of health, the match of the ego with its desire for Spirit has occurred. We embody the highest truth of our deep soul's yearning. Likewise, when a person suffers trauma in childhood or undergoes a long period of extreme stress, they can get stuck in the lower Levels of Development. By then it is likely they are very ill or incarcerated in some way.

As Don and Russ point out, most people tend to gravitate up and down within the Average Levels. Understanding how the personality fluctuates through these levels, sometimes as rapidly as daily depending on our circumstances, will help us identify our patterns. It also gives us a vision of our best selves that we can become as we gain understanding and self-awareness.

Centers of Perception

The Enneagram types can be grouped into three centers of perception, which Don Riso and Russ Hudson call Gut or Instinctive, Heart or Feeling, and Head or Thinking. All of us receive intuition energetically in different ways. We will either have a sense of perceiving life through our body, like having Gut intuition, or we'll perceive life through our Heart, a kind of heart-knowing, or we'll have this awareness seem to be in our Heads, as intuition. It is much more subtle (and powerful) than Gut types having a stronger body, Head types being smarter, or Heart types experiencing more love than others. Don and Russ point out in *Understanding the Enneagram* that though we have all three centers of perception within us, each of us will find that we gravitate toward a particular center in our awareness of life, and at the same time, we will tend to neglect one of them. The third center generally follows the most used center. Then the problem is that we end up "scrambling" the centers and using them in ineffective ways.[21] For example, we may take action without thinking clearly or make decisions based on our emotions. This results in our unconscious pattern, our "samscara" and thus, our Enneagram type.

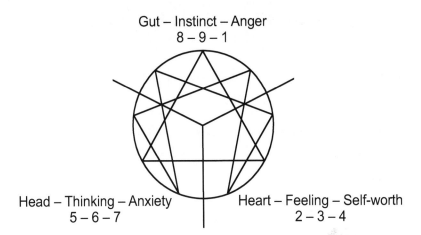

Gut – Instinct – Anger
8 – 9 – 1

Head – Thinking – Anxiety
5 – 6 – 7

Heart – Feeling – Self-worth
2 – 3 – 4

Three types in the Enneagram personality pattern have Gut perception: Type 8 the Leader, Type 9 the peacemaker and Type 1 the Reformer. Each of the Gut types has a focus on Anger issues in their lives; they each deal with anger energy in different ways.

Eight Leaders are very comfortable expressing anger and thrive on conflict and confrontation.

Nine Peacemakers get cut off from Gut energy and deny their anger. They seem to have none, but it festers and eventually blows.

One Reformers have an internal moral battle with their anger. It turns into resentment.

Three types in the Enneagram personality pattern have Heart perception: Type 2 the Helper, Type 3 the Achiever and Type 4 the Individualist. They each have issues of the heart, specifically of shame, self-criticism and questions of self worth.

Two Helpers move outward, seeking validation from others hoping to find the love they seek.

Three Achievers focus on ways to achieve success and validation in their world. When stressed, they get cut off from Heart awareness.

Four Individualists dive into deep emotional states to try to understand themselves.

Three types in the Enneagram personality pattern have Head perception: Type 5 the Thinker, Type 6 the Loyalist, and Type 7 the Enthusiast. These types are experts in mental anxiety, the "monkey-mind" chatter that often overwhelms them.

Five Thinkers move inward to study, thus reassuring themselves that they are mentally competent, thus avoiding anxiety.

Six Loyalists have an entire "committee" of anxious voices in their heads arguing with each other.

Seven Enthusiasts avoid the anxiety by floating above it. Go to the next Party.

Description of the Enneagram Types

The Peacemaker

The Challenger

The Reformer

The Enthusiast

The Helper

The Loyalist

The Achiever

The Investigator

The Individualist

Riso-Hudson Type Names

This next section is a brief overview of each type, a summary based on the teachings of Don Riso and Russ Hudson of the Enneagram Institute. For more detail about each type, I highly recommend all the Riso-Hudson books and their informative website.[22] The animal references are not from Riso/Hudson material, but are from the teaching of Dr. Mary Helen Keller at the Monastery of St. Clare in Memphis.[23] I think the animals are a fun way to illustrate some of the main traits of each type.

Type One - The Reformer (Eagle Vision)

The One, called the Reformer, is principled and idealistic. Ones have a strong sense of right and wrong and are very aware of how things should be done. Ones are often advocates for change and improvement. The Reformer's Passion is Resentment and their Basic Fear is of being corrupt, evil or defective. Interestingly, these two impulses are at odds with each other. To be angry is perceived by Ones as wrong or morally weak, so Ones have an uncomfortable truce with their feelings of anger and it comes out as righteous resentment. Because their Basic Desire is to be good and to have integrity, they are attuned to what needs to be right and they strive to be right. Though they often campaign for righteous causes, they can also degrade into critical narrow mindedness. A well organized, but over stressed Reformer can spiral into being critical both of himself and others, and perfectionistic to the point of paranoia.

When Ones are healthy, they are seen as discerning and noble. Gandhi, a well known Reformer, wrote at length about his struggle with anger and resentment. There is a scene in the movie Gandhi that illustrates this conflict with negative emotions and righteous passion. He asks his wife to take her turn cleaning the latrines, to be an example for his teaching that it's fair and right that everybody share in the duties usually reserved for the lowest caste. He reacts with anger and frustration when she resists and later feels guilty for his anger toward her and comes to her to apologize.

A Reformer with a Nine wing will be more introverted, often working toward excellence behind the scenes, whereas the Reformer with a Two wing will be more interpersonal and outgoing like the Helper Two Type.

When Reformers are stressed they become frustrated and depressed that there is so much wrong in the world and in themselves. Then they begin to experience the depression so common in Fours. Likewise, to follow the line in the other direction, the path to healing for Reformers is to lighten up and learn to play like the Sevens do naturally. What they can learn from the Individualist Fours however, is a deep sense of being with their negative emotions with equanimity.

Type Two - The Helper (Dog Devotion)

Helpers are caring, warm-hearted and loving at their best. They derive their sense of self from how much they love others. The problem with this is that they expect that this love will be returned. When this love isn't returned in kind, the Helper's very self image is shaken and shamed. Their Passion is Pride, because their ego gets caught in the idea that they alone know what someone needs, that they are able to care and give it to them. Because the Basic Fear of Twos is of being unwanted or unworthy of love, they give in order to receive. Their Basic Desire is to feel loved, and they achieve this by giving to others.

When a Helper is emotionally healthy, their attention to others is altruistic and unconditional. A dramatic example of the Helper's energy is Mother Teresa. In fact many people in helping or service careers are Twos. However, when Twos are stressed they become needy, possessive and co-dependent. If they feel that their offerings of service have been ignored or denied, over time they lose their sweetness and begin to act like the angry Eight.

Helpers are so focused on others' needs that they tend to neglect their own needs. Somatic illnesses such as Fibromy-algia are common, as their bodies attempt to claim some nur-turing and care. Their journey toward emotional health is to realize that they are inherently worthy and loved just as they are. The Integration line moves to the emotional wisdom and solitary insight of a healthy Individualist Four. Only after they have moved through this spiritual awakening, and all around the pattern, can they also experience the inner strength and bold big-hearted generosity characterized by Type Eight.

Twos with a One wing tend to direct their energy toward people or causes who might need them, as well as embody their ideals. Twos with a Three wing will be content to sit back and promote people and causes that they support.

Type Three - The Achiever
(Beaver Work Ethic or Peacock Charm)

Achievers are adaptable, success driven and charming. Their Basic Fear is of being worthless and they will therefore focus on whatever their family and culture values so that they can achieve their Basic Desire of feeling valuable and worthwhile. They are focused on whatever is seen as desirable, whether the stage is Hollywood or Wall Street. They will rise to the top, or die trying. The more stressed and emotionally unhealthy they become, the more they work and struggle competitively toward this goal of being recognized as valuable and of worth. Achievers have a knack for sensing what people want to hear or believe and they have a chameleon-like ability to deliver it. This leads to their Passion of Deceit in an effort to cover their shame, however subtle, as the truth becomes more and more blurry.

Yet when Achievers are emotionally healthy, they really are authentic and inspirational role models. They are leaders and culture changers. They inspire and help others to see the possibilities for greatness. They are willing to share their limelight and bring others into it. A wonderful example of this is Tony Robbins, a self-motivated success guru. Many politicians and public figures are Threes, so there are many examples of well-known Threes, both healthy and unhealthy.

When Threes are emotionally unhealthy, there is a break down in their drive for success and they collapse into that numbness so well known to Nines. When they are healthy they are able to keep a sense of humor around their competitive spirit and play well with others just like the "Six-pack." Since the Integration lines connecting to Threes, Nines and Sixes are shorter, this indicates the ease with which they can go into or out of balance.

When Achievers have a Two wing, their focus is more toward serving others in some way, such as in politics or business. Achievers with a Four wing are a bit more self-oriented and are more often found in creative or theatrical venues.

Type Four - The Individualist (Regal Cat)

Individualists are introspective and romantic, often living in their imaginations and getting lost in their emotions. Since their emotional states are always changing, their Basic Fear is that perhaps they have no identity or significance. They search to find and understand themselves, their Basic Desire. Their focus tends to drag down toward what is missing or lacking in their lives, while disregarding what they actually have. Their Passion is Envy. It is an envy of the soul, a denial of what one has, while longing for what is missing, both within themselves and in their environment.

Fours are deeply intuitive. The problem is that they often don't act on their intuition and possibilities, except inside their heads. So these possibilities pile up as unfinished potentials. Often they can't remember the difference between their imaginations and reality. Thus Fours have a tendency toward depression, exhaustion and feeling overwhelmed.

What saves Fours from this emotional self-destruction is to take action, applying their creativity to the physical world. They must get into their body by getting physical. This helps them see through the veil of the emotion and thus find Equanimity, the Fours gift of Spirit. Then Fours begin to incorporate the high qualities of the One type into their innate creativity: commitment to something higher outside themselves, the ability to take right action, think logically and make decisions, and the ability to stay on task.

Four Wing Three, the Aristocrat, has some of the Three's refined sense of style, the subtle ability to read other people and that competitive edge. Four Wing Five is more introverted and considers being "odd, strange or weird" a badge of character. They are called the Bohemians, often on the cusp of change and new trends or revolutions.

Type Five - The Investigator (Owl Vision)

Investigators are perceptive and cerebral. Their Basic Fear is of being useless, helpless or incapable. They are therefore driven to become knowledgeable about whatever will give them an intellectual edge in the world and help them feel competent. Fives are drawn to the unusual, the unique, the detailed and complicated. Though they forgo many material comforts and possessions, ironically they often have extensive collections or rare finds. Though Investigators are usually very introverted and shy, if you show an interest in their specialty, you will open them up. Their Basic Desire is to be capable and competent and to be seen as the expert.

Yet this hard-won competency is often limited by their inability or reluctance to take this knowledge from the mind and put it into action. The Investigator's Passion is Avarice which arises out of the desire to withhold this knowledge from others and use it to gain a feeling of usefulness. Emotionally healthy Fives finally realize that they do know enough and are able to come out of their studious shell to share it with others. They become leaders, speakers and teachers as they move along the Integration Line to embody the confidence of Type Eight. Unhealthy Fives often appear to be like Sevens, as their mental anxiety becomes more pronounced.

At their best, Fives are not only intellectual but often intuitive as well. They are able to see beyond the ordinary, making discoveries and seeing the world in a new way. A study of Einstein's life shows his progression from intellect to insight as he changed the way humanity viewed the universe. Not all Fives are equally brilliant, yet they all identify themselves as knowledge seekers. Fives with a Four wing will be even more connected to their intuition and emotion. Fives with a Six wing are more technical minded, more logical and analytical.

Type Six - The Loyalist (Wolf Pack)

Loyalists are committed to whatever and whoever supports their desire for security. This could take the form of a religious, political or social group or ideology. Their Basic Fear is being without support or guidance, so they latch on to what brings them security and support, their Basic Desire. Their Passion of Fear, or more specifically Fear of Faithlessness, drives them to join with causes, groups, beliefs and people who can offer security. Sixes are slow to trust, they cautiously and tentatively gauge every situation and relationship as to its capacity to be trust worthy. That said, once a Six makes a friend or joins a group, it is for life. Loyalists, while generally very cautious and meticulous, also have a "wild-side" when they test their loyalties, determining who and what to put their trust in.

Loyalists have a hard time with change and feel most comfortable with familiar patterns. They like to sit in the same seat, keep the same schedule and generally keep an orderly lifestyle. Loyalists also have a hard time making decisions. They are tuned in to imaginary scenarios of what could go wrong, but they are not that connected to their intuitions. They have an "inner committee" of authorities in their heads that they run every decision by over and over until they're dizzy with anxiety.

While Fours and Fives are comfortable with being solitary, Sixes, like wolves, like to run in a pack. They are playful, charming and caring (in tangible detail) with members of their pack. This playfulness and ability to see the dangers in the world combines with their inherent anxiety and results in delightful ironic wit. Many comedians are Loyalists. However, when anxiety increases into fear, Loyalists gravitate into "us against them" mentality. They become suspicious and reactive, and as a group can actually be dangerous.

Because of Loyalists' attention to detail and organization, they are excellent troubleshooters in any group. They are the "original boy scout" who remembers to bring, or has on hand, anything anyone might possibly need. Healthy Loyalists are quite courageous since they have had to overcome their own anxieties and fears.

Sixes with a Five wing are more introverted and cautious, while Sixes with a Seven wing combine their anxious wit with more physical and verbal action and are much more outgoing.

Type Seven – The Enthusiast
(Playful, Skillful Otter)

Enthusiasts are busy and productive, and seem to be perpetually happy. Wouldn't we all like to be Sevens? But it can be an illusion. The Enthusiast's Basic Fear is of being deprived or trapped in emotional or mental pain. Their Desire is to be satisfied, content and have their needs filled. Thus their Passion is called Gluttony, in which the desire to consume anything and everything that will distract them from feeling deprived and trapped in pain. A stressed-out Enthusiast just goes faster, rising to a manufactured happiness.

But when they are emotionally healthy, the Seven's spiritual Gift is Joy, and they have a natural optimism and playfulness. It's not an escape from reality but a natural and more relaxed acceptance of all that is uplifting.

When stressed, the Seven moves in the Direction of Disintegration to One. They realize they need to focus and deal with all their distractions; they then become impatient and critical like Ones. When healthy Sevens move in the Direction of Integration to Type Five, through self-awareness and inner work, they learn to slow down and quiet the mind. They go deep and stay with observations long enough to cultivate the inner knowing of wisdom.

Seven Wing Six, Entertainers, combine their high energy with organization, wit and an engaging style. They are able to accomplish a great deal and often have a wonderful sense of humor. Seven Wing Eight, the Realist, combines this high energy with strength and confidence. There is a sense of living on the edge; these are the race car drivers of the world. Most Sevens live in the Average Levels where a low level of tension resides with joy and results in busyness, restlessness, and distraction. Though they are acquisitive, scattered and tend toward excess they still seem to be having the most fun of all the personality types, hiding their pain with skill.

Type 8 - The Challenger (Powerful Tiger)

Challengers have a powerful, aggressive energy. Their Basic Fear is of being harmed or controlled by others. Often they have been in situations where they have themselves been controlled or abused and have decided to not let it happen again. Their Basic Desire is to protect themselves and be in control. This leads to the Passion of Lust as they exert their strength and control over others. If they are healthy, they will be champions of the underdog and those they love. They will take care of their own. If not healthy, a Challenger is armed and dangerous toward anything or anyone who threatens either themselves or "their people."

Healthy Eights move along the lines of Integration toward the energy of the Helper Two. When this happens, their desire to protect and lift up others turns into generous magnanimous service toward others. Challengers are like Mack trucks filled with marshmallows when you get to know them, as cracks in their armor become more visible. But when Challengers are stressed they move in the Direction of Stress toward Five and become more isolated, cynical and dark.

Challengers respect directness and boldness. They want a good argument and actually thrive on conflict. When confronting an Eight it is important to stand your ground even if it's scary. You will gain their respect. Once conflict is resolved, the Eight is over it. Challengers tend to become the leader in any group, even if they don't actively seek it. They fill up a room with their energy. They are grounded and are able get things done as they move through obstacles with energy and passion.

Eight with a Nine wing is an interesting mix. On one hand they crave conflict and intensity; on the other they avoid conflict. Eights with a Seven wing tend to be very energetic and bold, combining their passion with their anxiety.

Type 9 – The Peacemaker
(Bear: Winnie the Pooh AND Grizzly)

Peacemakers are easy-going and self-effacing. Nines seek peace and comfort at all costs, not by resolving issues but by avoiding them. Their Passion, Sloth, is a spiritual and mental inertia, while at the same time they can look quite busy on the surface. It doesn't mean that they are lazy, but that they begin to disassociate from life and begin to numb out to possible situations of conflict or become passive-aggressive.

Their Basic Fear is of loss and separation from a feeling of Unity and Harmony. Their Basic Desire is to have inner stability, or peace within themselves. Even when Peacemakers are stressed, they still retain their aura of peace and invisibility.

Since they are in the center of the Instinctual types, their Primary center is also their Unused center when they are unhealthy or stressed. What this means is that Nines can go radically from being in touch with instinctual energy and be very grounded, to getting stressed out and feeling disembodied in a very real sense. A Nine's favorite mantra is "I exist", which will probably only make sense to another Nine.

When unhealthy, Nines feel repressed, become neglectful and desolate, while at the healthy Levels they embody steadiness, harmony and indomitable quiet strength. Average Nines float along with life, kindly making no waves, while embodying Thoreau's quote, "most men live lives of quiet desperation."

The Nine's Direction of Integration is to Three, where they begin to realize their value and potential. They overcome inertia and their activities become more related to the real world. Then they are able to fully bring their Gift of Peace to others in an active, connected way.

When stressed the Nine's Direction of Disintegration is toward the anxiety of Six. They will turn passive-aggression into projects and activity, laced with paranoia and suspicion. Nines have to go through the inner growth and confidence gained by facing the conflicts in their lives.

Nine with an Eight Wing, the Referee, combines the placidity and gentleness of Nine with the strength and focus of Eight. Nine Wing One, the Dreamer, is able to synthesize many different points of view and see the relationships between them.

Patterns of the Enneagram END NOTES:

17. Most of the Riso-Hudson books expound on Passion, Fears and Desires as the primary motivations driving our personality patterns.

18. Wings are discussed in most of the Riso/Hudson books, particularly in *Wisdom of the Enneagram and Personality Types*.

19. Integration Lines are discussed in most of the Riso/Hudson books, particularly in *Personality Types* and *Understanding the Enneagram*.

20. *Personality Types* goes into the most detail in describing the Levels of Development for each type.

21. *Understanding the Enneagram*. The practical guide to personality types, how to use it in daily life and in many settings. Has a section on comparisons, helpful if you can't decide your type. Also has the **section that influenced this book about balancing the Centers**.

22. Enneagram Institute website: **www.enneagraminstitute.com**

23. *Enneagram Skins*. How the Enneagram personality types can be illustrated by animals. Dr. Mary Helen Keller. Monastery of St. Clare, Memphis, TN.

Questions for Self-Inquiry:

1. How would I describe myself? List up to 10 adjectives.

_____

_____

_____

_____

2. How would my friends describe me?

_____

_____

_____

_____

3. Which of these Enneagram types do I identify with?

_____

_____

_____

_____

4. Which of these Enneagram types do I not identify with?

_____

_____

_____

_____

Centers of Perception

Balancing the Centers

In Don Riso and Russ Hudson's book *Understanding the Enneagram*, they discuss how to find the balance of each of the three centers: Head, Heart and Gut. Finding this balance is important because the imbalance of the centers is actually the ultimate cause of the personality patterns. In other words, if we use our centers appropriately we will feel balanced and whole.

When these Centers are unbalanced two of the centers can become tangled and confused. We then often neglect the other (or third) center, and the result is a state of unbalance. Riso and Hudson have experienced that working with the third, or unused Center, is very helpful for most people of average health. Once awareness of the Unused Center is accessed, work can begin on the Second Center to further align the energy.[24]

Hornevian Coping Patterns

This pattern involves the grouping of types known as Hornevian, so named after the psychoanalyst Karen Horney (1885-1952), who described three different ways of coping with stress. Don Riso and Russ Hudson align a type in each of the Centers with one of these coping styles.[25]

The **Withdrawn** types, Four, Five and Nine, tend to move away from the stressor.

The **Compliant** types, One, Two, and Six, are compliant to either the cause of stress, or to their own super-ego dictates and ideals.

The **Assertive/Aggressive** type reacts by asserting back, against others or the environment, and is seen in type Three, Seven and Eight.

What each Hornevian category shares is a common Unused Center. As Riso and Hudson sum it up:

> "**Withdrawns** (Fours, Fives, and Nines)
> need to engage the body.
>
> **Compliants** (Ones, Twos, and Sixes)
> need to work with the quiet mind.
>
> **Assertives** (Threes, Sevens, and Eights)
> need to open the heart."[26]

Types Three, Six and Nine have an especially ironic situation in that the center that is often neglected is actually their Primary Center, the Center they use most when they are healthy. For this reason these types may experience more initial difficulty, but make rapid progress in finding balance.

This was particularly exciting to me because as a yoga instructor I knew that I could then recommend an optimal practice for each of my students based on these principles.

Both yoga and the Enneagram can be used together to balance the Centers and thus help us find freedom from the imbalances that cause us pain and confusion. The practice of yoga is directly related to balancing our Energetic Anatomy. The choice of particular postures, sequences and breath practices (pranayama) can be used to balance the Chakras, or Centers of the Enneagram.

The **first three Chakras** located in the pelvic area can be grouped together as the Gut Center. They deal with one's familial identity, a sense of being grounded, passion, the element of fire, and the energetic aspect of sex, power and money.

The **Fourth Chakra** in the Heart is the emotional center of the body. The **Fifth Chakra** in the throat relates to speaking one's truth and integrity; it may correspond to either or both the Heart center and the Head center.

The **Sixth Chakra** between the eyebrows, the center of intelligence and intuition, would correspond to the Head Center. The **Seventh Chakra** is an integration of all the other Chakras with spiritual awareness.

To bring this information to a useful plan of action for each Enneagram type, we begin by organizing the patterns into the Hornevian groups: **Withdrawn, Assertive, Compliant**.

Hornevian Groups

How We Respond to the World

Personality Type	How we respond	Work with the Unused Center
1, 2, 6	Compliant	Thinking
4, 5, 9	Withdrawn	Instinctual
3, 7, 8	Assertive	Feeling

1, 2, 6 * Work to develop the Thinking center: focus on calming the mind, develop intuition. **Yoga:** *forward bends, gentle inversions, meditation*

4, 5, 9 * Work to develop the Instinctual center: focus on developing energy, getting grounded. **Yoga:** *strong standing, balancing, abs, supine*

3, 7, 8 * Work to develop the Feeling center: focus on opening heart, connecting with emotions. **Yoga:** *backbends, supported poses, bhakti*

The Withdrawn Group –
Focus on Strength, Being in the Body

The Withdrawn group (Four, Five and Nine) has a tendency to get their Heart and Head tangled up, neglecting their Gut center. Thus, they tend to omit, or forget about their bodies. Fours think with their hearts, Fives feel with their minds and the Nines go numb.

These types benefit the most from strong grounding postures, such as warrior and fierce pose. The Ujjayi breath and the Kapalabhati / Bastrika (Fire) breath, which are both energizing and expansive, are especially valuable to this group. Deeply physical sequencing, such as the Ashtanga and Power yoga sequences or even slower powerful Vinyasa are effective for connecting to Gut energy. Holding difficult strengthening postures such as lunges, arm balancing poses, pushups and sit-ups is a valuable tool to help the Withdrawn group connect to the physical body.

This is the last thing they would want to do. However if they will do it, getting physical will allow the heart and mind to unwind and return to their appropriate place. Fours will be able to reframe distorted thinking patterns and perceptions, especially negative interpretations of self and others. Fives will be able to process their feelings, especially those of rejection and futility, and Nines will be able to release blocked energy in the body, especially repressed rage and fear.

Fours – The Individualist

As a Four, I have found that a strong physical practice is both essential and difficult to maintain. I have a tendency to think that I am practicing yoga, when in reality I have only been reading about it or thinking about it. I identify with the image of being a yogi and tend to neglect to actually do my practice. The most profound practice for a Four is simply just doing yoga regularly and assertively enough to make a difference. When the body is strong and grounded, the Individualist Four finds mental clarity is much easier to maintain and they are not dominated by their emotions so much.

Fives – The Thinker

Bob (all names have been changed) is a Five. He reads about yoga, about philosophy and spiritual things. He says he wants to come to class, but he just asks me what books I recommend. It's been over a year now, and I will be very surprised if he actually shows up.

I do have a few five students, who actually show up, and they are very intellectual, having a need to fully understand each aspect of their practice. They ask a lot of questions, read a lot of books and really do work hard. My observation is that they gain the most from deep physical work, which allows their emotional energy to disengage from mental activity and they are able to be more present.

Nines – The Peacemaker

My mom, a Nine, is one of my most enthusiastic students. Since beginning her yoga practice, she has become much more active and confident in every area of her life. In her late 60's, she frequently rode her bike 30 - 50 mile stretches and participated in a bikathon, completing 66 miles, her age at the time. I asked her what the hardest posture was for her. It was triangle, which is a standing, side stretch posture where the balance is awkwardly extended out to the side. Triangle brought up the sense of conflict, so it was emotionally uncomfortable. We have been working on this posture, and looking at how her reaction in triangle is similar to her reaction to conflict in life. As she has mastered this posture emotionally and physically, she has also experienced empowerment in life situations.

Nines tend to find balance quickly when they engage their Gut, Instinctual self. The Nine's favorite and easiest part of yoga practice is relaxation and meditation.

The Assertive Group –
Focus on Heart Opening, Emotional Connection

The Assertive group (Three, Seven and Eight) tends to engage the mind and gut, taking action where their minds direct them. They tend to close themselves off from the wisdom of their hearts when they are under stress. They benefit the most by opening the Heart Center, through backbends, by opening the chest in forward bends and through very gentle nurturing postures, such as child pose. This is often very hard for them to do, either physically or emotionally. They will either be very physically tight in this area, or they will be able to do the pose but will not be able to really connect with it.

Their minds are busy with thoughts of "what is next?" (Sevens), "am I doing it right or best?" (Threes).... or "I hate this pose!" (Eights), and they envelop themselves in thought rather than the experience of the posture. But if they persist and eventually allow themselves to fully explore the energy of backbends, it has an amazing effect on them. Backbends open up the Fourth Chakra, the emotional center. When a Three, Seven or Eight cries after my class or in yogic emotional release therapy, I know that something has really shifted; some emotional armor has been released.

Threes – The Achiever

Threes are in the center of the heart triad and are most easily connected and disconnected to the heart energy. The biggest challenge that Threes seem to have in yoga class is during the relaxation (Savasana - corpse pose). Up until the final relaxation, as long as there is something to do, the Three excels, often with an eye to the mirror to seek approval. During relaxation, however, the goal is to do nothing. To a Three, the idea of doing nothing is an incongruous waste of time. They are also often engulfed in powerful emotions the minute they remain quiet and receptive, so they will toss and turn and often find any excuse to leave. Once they realize how valuable this time is however, Threes will quickly be able to relax into the fulfillment of a beautiful, open Heart.

Sevens – The Enthusiast

I have quite a few Sevens in my classes. I think they find the spontaneity and creativity of my teaching style fun. I find that I have to challenge them to slow down and fully experience the moment, the breath and the emotions being released as they do their postures.

Jane is an enthusiastic Seven who comes regularly. She plows into everything head first and her biggest challenge is going slowly into difficult postures that require steady balance. So her balancing postures and headstands are a bit unsteady, but she is relentless and bold. She tells all her friends about yoga and often brings them to class. She brings a sense of fun and playfulness to the classroom, but she has often found a space of deep joy and emotional clarity in her yoga practice, especially after slow backbends.

Eights - The Challenger

Karen is a yoga teacher and she fills the room with her energy. She has been able to blend her steady strength with a nurturing gentleness that is endearing to her students. In her personal practice, she is working through the trepidation of backbends. Not fear, of course, because you know that Eights are not afraid of anything. It's more that to fully experience the backbend you have to give up some control, just let go and expand into the unknown and that is the difficulty for an Eight.

The Compliant Group –
Focus on Calm Mind, Open to Intuition

The Compliant group (One, Two and Six) is most out of touch with a calm mind and with confidence in their intuition. They take action based on their emotional state: One's with righteous anger, Two's with protective compassion or resentment, and Six's with fear and anxiety. The Compliant group benefits most by a slow, deep practice and a format that helps to focus the mind. Breathing with exhales twice as long as inhales and the "falling-out breath" help the body and emotions get untangled. Restorative (advanced lying around) postures help them learn to relax and receive. Inversions help them to see another point of view. Forward bends help them to release tension, while feeling enough tension in the hamstrings to focus the mind.

Ones – The Reformer

I have found that Ones have the most trouble being spontaneous and exploratory with their yoga. They want clarity and detailed direction. It would be a powerful practice for them to be able to explore and play with their practice intuitively, while the teacher provides a safe place in which to do so. It is probably no accident that the Iyengar style, a very structured form of yoga, emphasizes inversions (headstand, shoulder stand) which provide an upside-down point of view, energetically as well as physically, and thus help shake up rigid beliefs. Mr. Iyengar is probably a One, as are probably most of the top Iyengar teachers.

Twos – The Helper

There is a high percentage of type Two yoga instructors since Twos tend to be called into helping, nurturing professions like yoga. They are often personally drawn to do yoga because of some kind of system breakdown or stress reaction from neglecting their own needs. Fibromyalgia is a "Two-ish" condition. The challenge for a Two is to learn the importance of taking the time' for themselves. Simple self-care will feel very selfish and indulgent, and it usually takes a physical or mental crisis for Twos to realize the importance of self-care. Their direction is focused outward on others for connection, love and approval, so they have a difficult time really focusing inward for relaxation. Lots of indulgent restorative postures and gentle stretches will allow a Two to relax and find mental clarity, thus allowing them to take action that is grounded, appropriate and focused.

Joyce experienced this power of inward focus the weekend she participated in my first Ennea-yoga workshop. She came to the workshop despite the fact that she was in the middle of a very emotional crisis with her son. She felt that the school administration was using him to make a point to the other students. She resisted her mother-tiger (2 goes to 8) urge to march down to the school with a bazooka and instead spent the weekend doing yoga. Afterward, she was able to calmly organize a plan and communicate with lawyers, her husband and other parents who were involved. The situation was resolved and her relationship with her son was greatly improved. Having a calm mind helped her to act in a more effective way.

Sixes – The Loyalist

Sixes do well in a nurturing environment with a teacher who has earned their trust. They quickly realize the power of yoga to quiet the mind, thus unscrambling their propensity for anxiety. Sixes are often very cautious physically; they need reassurance from a trusted guide to bolster their confidence. Gentle stretches and slow deep breathing help the Six to let go of chronic anxiety. They gain confidence in themselves as they try challenging postures, and eventually they learn to trust themselves. Sixes are also very steady in their practice; they will show up as scheduled. We have a bit of a joke at my studio: that after closing and moving the studio several times, the only students left who have followed me from place to place are Sixes!

Working with the Second Center

After the neglected center has been brought into balance, the next step according to Riso and Hudson is to focus on the Second Center, which may still be somewhat tangled and confused with the First Center. We see this pattern in the Harmonic Groupings, labeled Competency, Emotional Realness (formerly called Reactive) and Positive Outlook. Here the types are grouped according to their different reaction styles.[27]

The **Competency group** is so named because their natural reaction is toward solving the problem. Ones do it right, Threes do it best, and Fives study it thoroughly. They will now be able to work on opening up the Heart and accessing their feelings. The **Emotional Realness group** is so named because they tend to react emotionally to problems. The Fours will do it with drama, Sixes with fear, and Eights with anger. To balance their Second Center it will be important to cultivate a quiet mind. The **Positive Outlook group** reacts positively in various ways. Twos are drawn to help, the Sevens tend to avoid the problem ("not my problem"), and the Nines maintain a blissful, but intentional, unawareness of the problem. They will now find that getting grounded and accessing their Gut Center will liberate their energy.

The **Competency group** (One, Three and Five) will discover that as they work on their specific Unused Center, their common Second Center, the Feeling center, opens. If they courageously allow themselves to fully experience grief and other blocked feelings that are emerging, they will be able to fully own their spiritual gift or Essence: moral clarity (One), open heart (Three) and deep insight (Five).

The **Emotional Realness group** (Four, Six and Eight) will now experience the need to quiet the mind. As a four, I have experienced this process in yoga. I approach the practice initially with my heart, but I will not be able to quiet my mind until I have first connected with my body. Once I connect physically however, I am more available to the power of practices that quiet the mind. I then find that my emotions are no longer pulling me around. Likewise, the Six will relax further and become empowered. The Eight will open up to a deep tenderness of heart as they move into quiet, calming practices.

The **Positive Outlook group** (Two, Seven and Nine) will find that connection with the body, the Gut Center, is the next step, allowing the Two to experience deep relaxation, the Seven to experience an open heart and the Nine becomes more fully physically grounded. It is important to notice that in the Primary types (Three, Six and Nine) the center to work with is the same as their primary center, thus they have the most direct path of integration.

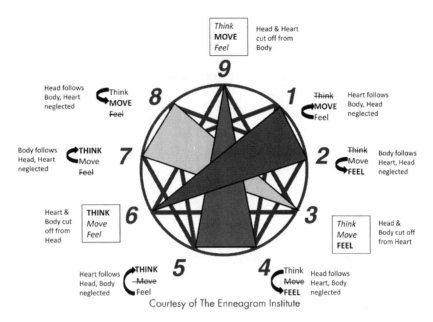

Courtesy of The Enneagram Institute

**Adapted from chart from Understanding the Enneagram
by Don Riso and Russ Hudson, Page 255.**

I have been using the Enneagram in conjunction with Phoenix Rising Yoga Therapy and Meditation. In this therapy, the client goes into a deeply relaxed state with deep breathing under the therapist's guidance. The therapist then lifts and holds their body in a variety of yoga positions. In this deeply meditative state, the client is encouraged to observe the mental and emotional releases, which occur as the postures are held. The therapist begins facilitating the inner dialogue of the client, with the idea that both awareness of the body and of Spirit offer wisdom and insight, when one is available to this kind of deep relaxation.[28] The experience is often quite revealing and liberating. Knowing the Enneagram type of my client has been especially powerful in this process.

The Three, Six and Nine types, which are at the center of each Head, Heart and Gut triad, have a unique path in that their Unused Center is also their Primary Center. It is more beneficial for them to let their other centers combine to bring them into a practice that focuses on their Primary Center. For example, a Nine uses her heart (desire for love and unity) with her mind (innate peacefulness) to help her come into her body. Once there she develops it and strengthens it, bringing about balance and integration.

In summary, a yoga practice can be organized according to type to help one find balance. Certain postures, breathing techniques, or even approaches to the practice affect the Chakras, or Centers, in specific ways. My yoga proposal, based on the Riso-Hudson recommendation, is that you go into your practice with the Primary Center, letting it inspire and draw you in. Then work toward achieving a sense of mastery and balance with your Unused Center. Finally work with your Second Center.[29] In the next section I develop a yoga practice with this theme in detail for each type.

Centers of Perception END NOTES:

24. *Understanding the Enneagram.* Chapter 7, pgs. 247-283, The Centers. Riso and Hudson based their understanding of the Centers in turn from the teachings of Gurjieff.

25. Karen Horney, a psychiatrist who developed the Freudian-based categories of conflict resolution, is discussed in several of the Riso-Hudson books. The term "Hornevian Groups" was coined by Riso-Hudson.

26. *Understanding the Enneagram*, pg. 277

27. *Understanding the Enneagram*, pg. 278

28. Phoenix Rising website: **www.pryt.com**

29. *Understanding the Enneagram*, The Centers, ch.7.

Recommendations for Each Type

One – The Reformer: Idealist, Advocate – Integrates to 7

Relax and Have Fun

The Reformer is also called Idealist and Advocate. They tend to get wrapped up in critical resentments and frustrated anger at all that isn't right in the world. They have a deep desire to be morally right. If you identify yourself as a One, you might be noticing that most of your stress revolves around frustration and criticisms, both of yourself and others. The lines of integration for Ones point to Type Seven, therefore the path to health for Reformers is to lighten up, relax and have fun. In the Reformer pattern, the Head is the Unused Center, so doing calming postures such as forward bends, supported inversions and meditation are important, as well as simply approaching your practice in a calm, light-hearted way.

Ones will be very comfortable with the precision and alignment detail of the Iyengar method. They will be very correct in doing the postures and it will be important to them to understand the proper form. Ones with a Nine wing will be diligent students, while Ones with a Two wing are very likely drawn to teaching, becoming inspiring and passionate teachers. One's gifts are integrity and discipline. The challenge for them will be in seeing that there are many ways, just as beneficial, to approach yoga. They must beware of the tendency to become too limited to the idea of the perfect posture or that a particular yoga style is the only right one.

My recommendation for Ones is to try new approaches, to strive for mental flexibility, not just the physical. Hang out with those adventurous Sevens and sample a variety of styles or ways of practicing. Perfection is not always in the usual form. The most edgy and valuable styles might be Vanda Scaravelli's method of going into postures only part of the way[30] or a Vinyasa flow class which emphasizes playful exploration and experimentation. Eric Schiffman's teaching is a good example of playful flow.[31]

As far as individual postures go, perhaps it is no accident that the Iyengar style emphasizes inversions. On a metaphysical level inversions bring one into a different perspective. Ones will find value in the meditative aspect of yoga, and especially pranayama that emphasizes the exhale, to help unwind mentally. The next step is to allow the heart to open by focusing on backbends and chest expansive postures. Experiment, dance and try new things.

Details for Ones

The Primary center is the **Gut**. Approach your yoga practice with body awareness, connecting to your physical strength and vitality. Your body is intuitive and you can sense this through your gut. You might start your practice by doing something grounding like a few pushups or sit-ups. Then sit quietly and see what happens next.

Focus on the Unused center, the **Head**. Cultivate this with a steady, mental focus and quieting postures such as child pose, legs up the wall or a forward bend. Your practice could focus on forward bends and inversions. Keep a slow, steady pace.

Practice Drishti, which is keeping a soft, focused gaze as you do your practice. Let your eyes follow the direction of your head but keep an inward focus. As the eyes relax, so does the mind. Be sure to include a variety of Pranayama and meditation. Breathwork should include a lot of the calming techniques, such as extended exhales or adding a pause, or retention, after the exhale.

Finish with the Second center, the **Heart**. Your practice can culminate in gentle, supported backbends to experience the open heart that will unfold at this point. Another option is chanting or something prayerful.

Meditation for One – Reformers

Focus on Universal Holy Perfection.[32] All things are in perfect order and are unfolding according to a Divine Plan. You can relax into that Perfection because there is nothing to do or fix. Consciously let go of any resentments about what is wrong with the world, and wrong with you. Visualize a beautiful stained glass with light shining through it. All the many colors make up the beauty and perfection of the vision. So it is with life. All is well and so are you. You are always in the Right Place at the Right Time, experiencing the Right thing. You were already forgiven. Experience the Serenity of that knowledge.

Results: Clarity and a relaxed mind; a shift to the Joy of Seven

Type 1 – Questions for Self-Inquiry:

1. What postures do I like? Why?

_____

_____

_____

_____

2. What postures do I dislike? Why?

_____

_____

_____

_____

3. Are the reasons for your liking or disliking a particular posture more physical or emotional or something else?

_____

_____

_____

_____

4. Does my self-talk during practice have a common theme? If so what is it?

_____

_____

_____

_____

Two – The Helper: Servant, Host(ess) – Integrates to 4

Nurture Yourself

The Helper is also called Servant or Host(ess). They are in the Heart Triad, but like Ones, tend to get out of touch with Head awareness. In other words, Heart goes forth with Gut and loses the calm mind of Head center. If you identify yourself as a Two, you might find yourself taking care of everybody else, with the unconscious desire to feel loved. Therefore, the lines of integration move to Type Four, and to regain your health you'll have to learn to nurture yourself. Find that Love that YOU ARE within your Self. It is straight from Source and you don't have to seek it from others.

Twos are very likely to be drawn to a guru or strong supportive teacher, but they should be careful to notice any tendency to become dependent or obsessively helpful, observing the motivations behind this. Twos are often found in healing professions or become therapists of some kind. Compassionate nurturing and unconditional love are your Gifts. But it is very important for twos to learn to receive, to pamper themselves and connect with Divine Love within. When they do this they will not be looking outside for validation from others because they will find it within themselves.

Lots of restorative postures, like child pose and legs up the wall pose are imperative for twos, especially if you are a care giver. Take regular personal retreats and look for any opportunity to develop your internal resources for nurturing yourself. As you use yoga first to find mental clarity, you will then find that strong, grounding postures will strengthen and help you find balance. Twos will find great sustenance in Bakti yoga, the yoga of Devotion, and will naturally bring a sense of devotion to their practice.

Details for Twos

Begin with the Primary center, your **Heart**: Approach your practice with receptive gratitude and devotion, which comes naturally. Start with a meditation, a prayer, child pose or a passive backbend.

Focus on the Unused Center, the **Head**, with steady, mental focus (drishti) and quieting postures. Cultivate a practice that focuses on forward bends, inversions and lots of supported passive postures, such as child pose, supported twists and forward bends. Keep it gentle. Focus on slow, deep breaths. This is just like what Ones need to do except that the theme is more about Nurturing Self-Care, than Clarity. Keep your mental gaze focused on your heart to quiet the mind.

Pranayama should include a lot of the calming techniques, such as extended exhales and pausing after the exhales. Do devotional Japa, which is meditation with a mantra, and focus on an image of the Divine. By the way, a mantra doesn't have to be in another language or given to you by a guru. Try some verse or phrase that is meaningful to you, for example: "Thy Love endures forever."

Finish with the Second center, the Instinctive **Gut** Center. Feel the strength of your body. You can enjoy a deep physical practice, increasing your strength and endurance, if you feel both clear and calm first. Take time after practice to be in the body, and take this awareness into your daily actions.

Meditation for Two – Helpers

You do not have to do anything, because you yourself are Divine Love, inside and out. It will flow through you naturally when you feel it from within, so simply bask in Love. Center your mind on something or someone you love. Chant the names of God or sing praises to God. The focus can be on Holy Will because now Love acts and you don't have to; Holy Freedom because you are free and open to this Love.

Results: Deep mental relaxation; experience of the creativity and individuality of a shift to Four.

Type Two – Questions for Self-Inquiry:

1. What postures do I like? Why?

_____

_____

_____

_____

2. What postures do I dislike? Why?

_____

_____

_____

_____

3. Are the reasons for your liking or disliking a particular posture more physical or emotional or something else?

_____

_____

_____

_____

4. Does my self-talk during practice have a common theme? If so what is it?

_____

_____

_____

_____

Three – The Achiever: Star, Professional – Integrates to 6

I am Not the Doer

The Achiever is also called the Star or the Professional. There is a common theme in yoga which is to practice Being, not Doing. This is a good mantra for Threes, who are often so focused on Doing, hoping to increase their perceived value. Threes are in the Heart Triad, yet when they feel stressed, their tendency will be to shut down the heart. The integration line of Type Three moves to Six, the Loyalist, so it is important to relax, just like Sixes need to, and to find faith in others and in Divine Source. You can't "win" it by Doing, so just Be.

Threes are probably too busy to come to a yoga class anyway, though sheer exhaustion may drive them there. They will find yoga to be the key to their stamina and success. They will most likely find a vigorous class to be the most fulfilling and they'll see the physical results. They may have a strong urge to leave class early before the final relaxation (savasana). On the surface it looks like you're not doing anything in relaxation, but this is actually the most valuable time in their practice. In yoga you never really "get there" or arrive, a deeper level of exploration always awaits. So Threes have to learn to enjoy the journey and give themselves recognition for their efforts. Remind yourself that yoga is not competition and to resist the urge to watch yourself in the mirror.

Keep learning with a "beginner's mind." A healthy Three has a big heart and can easily focus on the beauty and grace of the moment.

Details for Threes

Although the **Heart** center is a Three's Primary center, it is also often the Unused Center. Your purpose here is to find it. So begin with your mind and your body. Set an intention and get grounded. Do vigorous flow or strong standing postures.

Keep focusing on the **Heart**. Once you are focused and grounded, begin to put backbends into your practice. Focus on opening your heart. With every inhale, expand your chest. Your practice should include, and maybe alternate between as needed, both strong backbends and also the slow, gentle, supported backbends.

The pranayama that connects you to the Heart would be a deep 3-part inhale diaphragmatic breath, or any breath with emphasis on the inhale, lengthening the inhale or holding the breath after inhale. The meditation, of course, is to practice being and not doing. Practice "no-technique." Just observe.

Another possibility is to do a Gratitude practice: think of all the things that come to mind that you are grateful for and breathe in as you focus on them. Allow the memory of them to fill your heart.

Continue with what you find when you open your heart. Know that you have the time and you have the invitation to be with whatever you experience. Open your heart some more and be available to what you find there.

Meditation for Three – Achievers

Visualize a radiant column of sparkling light coming down through the crown of your head and filling you with Light. Divine Magnificence and Beauty are flowing through you and you don't have a thing to prove. Focus on Holy Law taking charge of what needs to be done and Holy Hope that it is done well. Relax into Radiant Beingness, "I am not the Doer."

Results: Opening the heart to the deep faith of Six, you become the solid covenant of faith that you were seeking.

Type Three – Questions for Self-Inquiry:

1. What postures do I like? Why?

_____

_____

_____

_____

2. What postures do I dislike? Why?

_____

_____

_____

_____

3. Are the reasons for your liking or disliking a particular posture more physical or emotional or something else?

_____

_____

_____

_____

4. Does my self-talk during practice have a common theme? If so what is it?

_____

_____

_____

_____

Four – The Individualist: Aristocrat, Bohemian – Integrates to 1

Just Do It

The Individualist is also called the Aristocrat and the Bohemian. Fours live in the Heart Center and are often so absorbed in their emotions that they have a hard time actually taking action in the world. The lines of integration for a Four indicate that they need to cultivate the passionate right action and focus of the Reformer. If you are an Individualist, let your Heart inspire you and then take planned action in that direction, no matter what mood you are in at the time. The Nike logo "just do it" is a great mantra for you.

Fours have the ability to bring light into the darkness, to inspire, bring a vision of Spirit to others from their experience of yoga. But this is really only possible if they actually get on the mat and do the practice. It is important for them to develop consistency and discipline in their life and it would be ideal to have a daily practice at the same time every day. This is the hardest thing on earth for a Four to do. For this reason, they may find it difficult to advance physically to more difficult postures. They must beware of adding guilt to the emotional mix about this.

Yoga for a Four should emphasize strong, grounding, standing and balancing poses. The Kundalini style of yoga, or Breath of Fire, will help them avoid depression and strengthen the immune system. The Vinyasa (Flow) style offers them a vehicle for creativity in their practice. Supine postures will bring stability. Plenty of Relaxation and Pranayama will stabilize emotions. Although consistency is imperative, creativity is a given and a strong yoga practice will enhance and channel their creativity. It is important though, for a Four to find a consistent, stable mentor to help them keep on track emotionally. Four yoga teachers can be very creative and inspiring, able to support students going through deep experiences.

Details for Fours

Let your Primary Center, your **Heart**, motivate you to begin your practice. Remember what doing your practice felt like last time. Remember how important and beneficial it has been for you. Fours tend to focus on what is missing so bring a sense of Gratitude to your mat; take time to remember your blessings.

Find your Unused Center, your body, the center of your **Gut** intuition. Make your focus be a strong physical practice with lots of standing postures, challenging and weight-bearing postures. Sweat. Play upbeat music to inspire you. Work up to backbends, balancing poses and anything that challenges you physically. Just Do It.

The best breathing techniques would be a strong dia-phragmatic Ujjayi (breathing across the throat to make a soft sound) breath, Kapalibhati or Bhastrika (Breath of Fire – Kundalini Yoga) to energize, and even Nadi Shodanam (alternate nostril breath) to balance energy. When they are depressed, Fours should focus on the inhale. And when they are feeling overwhelmed, the focus should be on exhales. Concerning meditation, just pick one method and Do It. Fours have a tendency to want to try everything and then do noth-ing, so again: just pick something and do it regularly for a while.

Now your Second Center comes into play, the calm **Mind**. Take time for supported relaxation, savasana and meditation. Allow your mind to clear, now that your emotions are quiet and your body strong and relaxed. Make intentions and set goals for your life only after being in this state, so that your decisions are grounded and not overly influenced by your mood.

Meditation for Four – Individualists

Visualize a primordial Divine force creating everything in perfection, love and amazing variety. You are a beloved part of this Holy Origin, created to flow with it and make it manifest in the material world. Open your heart and visualize being filled to the brim with this Creativity. Let go of self-criticism and let yourself move with whatever inspiration comes to you. To find that equanimity of emotional balance, when emotions come and go, say to yourself, "This too shall pass – only the Dance of Life, the Divine Creativity, remains."

Results: Grounded discipline and steadiness, beyond emotions of the moment in a shift to One. "Be the change you want to see in the world" Gandhi (a One).

Type Four – Questions for Self-Inquiry:

1. What postures do I like? Why?

_____

_____

_____

_____

2. What postures do I dislike? Why?

_____

_____

_____

_____

3. Are the reasons for your liking or disliking a particular posture more physical or emotional or something else?

_____

_____

_____

_____

4. Does my self-talk during practice have a common theme? If so what is it?

_____

_____

_____

_____

Five - The Investigator: Iconoclast, Problem Solver - Integrates to 8

Learn from your Experience

The Investigator is also called the Iconoclast and the Problem Solver. Fives live in their heads, and like the Fours, they tend to forget they have a body. When they integrate to their Gut – Intuitive center, they find empowerment at Type Eight, the Leader. If you are a Five, you may find that you dive into reading, study and more study, in order to escape an underlying anxiety within yourself. So the message here is that you probably know enough by now. Really, you do. Now it's time to get up and move. Learn also by doing. This is the opposite approach from a Three, if you remember.

Any type of yoga, or any exercise for that matter, will get a Five into their body, which will give them power and energy. To combat that underlying anxiety, Fives also need the time and the space to explore their sensations and feelings in a safe environment. They must resist the urge to have to know everything about yoga first, and just like the Fours, they just have to do it, not over-think it. A famous Ashtanga teacher, Patabi Jois, once said, "yoga is 99% practice and 1% theory."

Meditation and pranayama will also be very important to help you get calm and understand the workings of your mind, but their benefits are available only after you've grounded yourself with a strong physical practice. This will be the Fives edge, because a Five is more likely to want to study yoga than to actually do the practice. Fives will probably be drawn to Viniyoga, Iyengar, or the study of Sanscrit and Raja Yoga (yoga of knowledge), because of the scientific depth in these paths. Like Ones they appreciate the form and detail, but also the variety of applications to various needs and abilities. However, unlike Ones, but just like Fours, they will be resistant to actually doing the practice. Fives can lend their skill to the much needed research on yoga's many benefits. When Fives are ready for a real growing edge, they could try the intimacy of partner yoga or Kripalu yoga, which emphasizes the observation of emotional release through the body. These are particularly challenging for Fives because they are very sensitive and intuitive, yet can be closed off from the Heart as well as the Gut when stressed.

Details for Fives

Begin with the Primary Center: the **Mind**. Let your studies of the yoga tradition inspire you to begin your practice. Visualize the benefits you will receive. You intellectually and probably intuitively know what to do. Doing Buddhist based mindfulness meditation may feel like a natural way to get centered.

Focus on the Unused Center, the **Gut**. In other words, get physical! Like fours, fives need a strong physical practice,

standing postures, abdominal core work and other challenging weight-bearing postures. This will bring their internal experience out into the physical world.

Go ahead and explore a variety of meditation and breath
techniques. The best breathing technique at first might be
the Falling out breath, just to get relaxed mentally. Once you
are centered, practice strong deep breath techniques, such
as Ujjayi, while engaging the Bandhas (engaging pelvic and
abdominal muscles). Like Fours, Kundalini based breathing,
such as Kapalibhati and Bastrika, will increase your Gut energy. Also, practice doing expansive breaths like the 3-part
inhale and simply focusing on the inhale with opening movements.

Finish with the Second Center, the **Heart**. Work up to backbends in your practice. Feel your chest lift even when out in
daily life, and your very posture and presence will change.
Open your heart. See how long you can stand being so open
and receptive. Others will notice your confident sense of
mastery and will ask you for advice.

Meditation for Five – Thinkers

Focus on Holy Omniscience, that Source of all knowledge and that all is known through Source. Relaxing into that clarity, you will have all the information you need when you need it. There is a song that goes, "We can all know everything without ever knowing why, it's in every one of us, you and I." Imagine yourself as a crystal clear vessel full of light, energy and wisdom. Visualize the energy, light and intelligence of a supernova, and image yourself in it.

Results: Deep insight and strength with a move to 8, intelligence will deepen into insight and intuition and this will give you confidence.

Type Five – Questions for Self-Inquiry:

1. What postures do I like? Why?

_____

_____

_____

_____

2. What postures do I dislike? Why?

_____

_____

_____

_____

3. Are the reasons for your liking or disliking a particular posture more physical or emotional or something else?

_____

_____

_____

_____

4. Does my self-talk during practice have a common theme? If so what is it?

_____

_____

_____

_____

Six – The Loyalist: Defender, Buddy – Integrates to 9

Find Your Haven

The Loyalist is also called the Defender and the Buddy. Loyalists are in the Center of the Head – Thinking Center, yet when they are stressed, a calm clear mind is the first to go. The yoga concept of "monkey-mind" is well-known to Sixes. To find that calmness, Sixes need to integrate to the Peace of Nine by cultivating a calming, yet strengthening practice. Connection to Source for a Loyalist is like a deep Haven, a Divine harbor of safety and security.

Sixes will enjoy the regularity of a consistent routine with a confident teacher with whom they feel safe. It is important for them to relax the mental chatter with an "everything's all right" mantra and the falling out breath, and do lots of comforting visualization and restorative postures to head off anxiety. Sixes might be inclined to learn everything about yoga so that they will feel comfortable with it, but must remember that real self-confidence comes from surrendering, letting go. They have to dive into the unknown. If they move slowly and steadily into more challenging postures, such as inversions and arm balances, mastering these will give them a deep self-confidence and courage. The supported variation of Savasana, propped up on blankets, is a valuable way to enter into relaxation if their tendency is to panic. Sixes will also enjoy the yoga community and being included in like-minded gatherings.

Details for Sixes

Although the Primary center is the **Head**, Sixes can begin by first integrating their hearts with their actions, accessing their other centers, **Heart** and **Gut**. Make an intention before practice and start with a comforting ritual that is meaningful to you.

Maintain a steady physical practice, and explore your ability to relax in even the challenging postures. Observe the breath and keep it steady. Try difficult things one step at a time. Learning to relax no matter what, in any posture, will develop your confidence. After a warm-up practice, focus on forward bends / Supported Inversions leading to long supported Savasana and meditation.

Breathing should begin with simple falling out breaths and deep diaphragmatic breath. Focus on relaxing by lengthening the exhales. End practice with strong, courageous Ujjayi breaths.

Stay with your inward focus; allow your mind to relax completely. Trust your experience. Listen to the inner confident voice of intuition.

Meditation for Six – Loyalists

Focus on a Holy Faith that is rock solid. Imagine laying in the sun on a strong rock or imagine being rocked in a giant Divine hammock. Opening yourself to Source will give you the faith, confidence and certainty you crave. Instead of beliefs and hopes, those are just of the mind, come into the NOW of the present moment and relax into it. Notice when your fear and worry take you into the past or future and come back into the Now.

Results: Empowerment and peace with a move to the harmony of Nine.

Type Six – Questions for Self-Inquiry:

1. What postures do I like? Why?

_____

_____

_____

_____

2. What postures do I dislike? Why?

_____

_____

_____

_____

3. Are the reasons for your liking or disliking a particular posture more physical or emotional or something else?

_____

_____

_____

_____

4. Does my self-talk during practice have a common theme? If so what is it?

_____

_____

_____

_____

Seven – The Enthusiast: Entertainer, Realist – Integrates to 5

Stick With It – Dive Deep

The Enthusiast is also called the Entertainer or the Realist. They are in the Head Triad, yet are very active physically since they are responding physically to their mental anxiety. Sevens avoid emotional pain by staying above it, so the path of integration is to stay with uncomfortable emotions and go deep. They will then integrate to the intuitive wisdom of healthy Fives. Like Threes, Enthusiasts tend to close off their hearts, so a heart-opening practice is beneficial.

Sevens can be enthusiastic yogis. They may have already been to all the classes and studied with all the teachers in the area. Or they may dabble a little and be turned off by the depth and discomfort of the practice. But if a Seven loves yoga, they really Love yoga. Their enthusiasm is inspiring to others – they will bring friends to class too. It would benefit them, however, to stick to one style or one teacher who they can be loyal to and study with consistently. Sevens would benefit by mastering one method or a difficult posture, maybe a balancing posture. If they are athletic, they would enjoy Astanga or Power Vinyasa classes. Sevens have little self-doubt to get in the way, so they will have a natural confidence and ability. Their edge however, would be slowing down to experience the emotional and spiritual depth of a yoga practice. Yoga will ultimately bring them in touch with their inner self, painful parts included. A challenging style would be Kripalu yoga with its focus on a deep emotional connection and slow movements.

Details for Sevens

Begin with your Primary center: the **Head** center. Dive into your practice with focus and enthusiasm. Do a broad thorough warm-up so that the mind is calm and the body is warm in preparation for deeper heart-opening work. Pranayama recommendations would include deep diaphragmatic breathing first just to get mentally centered. Then focus on keeping the breath slow and notice your tendency to speed up.

Next focus on the Unused center: the **Heart**. Slow down your practice; stay in each posture longer than is comfortable and notice what happens. Notice your impulse to skip on to the "next one." To open the heart focus on backbends and then long nurturing supported postures. Be with any emotions that arise. Breathe slowly. Take time for a very long relaxed savasana. Notice any agitation. What do you feel?

Finish with the Second center: the **Instinctual-Gut** center. With your heart open to Joy and your mind calm, take time to be present in your body. Feel each moment and be aware of the fullness of each moment.

Meditation for Seven – Enthusiasts

Can you find Joy without giddiness? Visualize Joy seeping deep down into your bones. There is a Holy Plan and you don't have to plan it or figure it out; it will find you. Float down the stream. Imagine flowing in a cosmic river of Joy, just playing in the flow. Let yourself be saturated in the flow of relaxed Joy.

Results: a focused, relaxed mind with access to the creative insight of a Five.

Type Seven – Questions for Self-Inquiry:

1. What postures do I like? Why?

_____

_____

_____

_____

2. What postures do I dislike? Why?

_____

_____

_____

_____

3. Are the reasons for your liking or disliking a particular posture more physical or emotional or something else?

_____

_____

_____

_____

4. Does my self-talk during practice have a common theme? If so what is it?

_____

_____

_____

_____

Eight – The Challenger: Maverick, Bear – Integrates to 2

Let Go Into Bliss

The Challenger is also called the Maverick or the Bear. Eights are in the Gut-Instinctive triad, thus are strong and grounded physically but, like Sevens, they tend to neglect their Heart Center when stressed. Eights are often called "mac trucks filled with marshmallows", since they integrate to the unconditional love of the Helper – Two when relaxed and healthy. The Challenger has a natural desire to be in control, but to awaken to Source, they have to let go and surrender.

Eights may find the surrender involved in yoga to be difficult. By this I mean both the surrender of the physical postures and the surrender to the leadership of the teacher. Deep stretches, both forward bends and back bends, assist the Eight in letting go and relaxing. A profound practice for the Eight is to be gentle to themselves, finding the gentleness within themselves. To practice trusting their teacher or to practice Karma yoga (kind action) anonymously are also ways to let go.

Eights often come to yoga with a natural innate strength and confidence. They have a natural ability in strong postures such as the warrior variations, chair-fierce pose and postures requiring upper body strength. They can become charismatic and magnanimous teachers if healthy, in fact many famous spiritual teachers are Eights, but they must be careful of the ego's desire for control.

Details for Eights

Begin with the Primary center: the **Instinctual-Gut** center. You'll be able to move into your practice with a solid sense of being grounded. This is a stable place to start. From this initial strength, begin to focus on bringing flexibility to the spine. Though forward bends will help you to surrender energetically, continuing into backbends will open your heart.

Focus your practice on the Unused center: the **Heart** center. Wind down with slow gentle restorative postures. Allow yourself the time for a long relaxation and meditation. Supported backbends are especially valuable.

Lengthen the exhale helps to still the ego. Other pranayama might emphasize falling out breaths, deep diaphragmatic breathing, and the cooling Sitali (inhaling through the tongue) breath.

By the end of this practice you will be accessing your Second Center: the **Head**.

You'll feel calm and centered, authentically and inwardly strong.

Meditation for Eight – Challengers

The Holy Truth of power is that there is nothing to move against or control because All is One. All is One. Just focus on the idea that All is One. Notice that all the weakness, ignorance and anger in the world is simply a forgetting of this experience of Oneness. Let your compassion for those who have forgotten this fill up your heart with softness and forgiveness.

Results: Tenderness of Heart in a shift to Two.

Type Eight – Questions for Self-Inquiry:

1. What postures do I like? Why?

_____

_____

_____

_____

2. What postures do I dislike? Why?

_____

_____

_____

_____

3. Are the reasons for your liking or disliking a particular posture more physical or emotional or something else?

_____

_____

_____

_____

4. Does my self-talk during practice have a common theme? If so what is it?

_____

_____

_____

_____

Nine – The Peacemaker: Referee, Dreamer – Integrates to 3

Facing It is Easier than You Think

The Peacemaker is also called the Referee and the Dreamer. Though they are in the center of the Gut-Instinctive Triad, when stressed they tend to neglect their bodies, much like Fours and Fives. They go numb, so that they can separate themselves from a sense of conflict and stay in their preferred peaceful place. Their path of integration then is to the assertiveness of the Achiever-Three, where they come alive and bring their inherent peace out into the world of conflict. Then they are able to access their natural strength and harmonious groundedness.

Much of yoga practice is about "playing the edge", which is confronting the conflict in the body and learning to relax anyway. Since Nines are already one with everything, they would prefer to skip right on over to the meditation part. If Nines practice going gently and steadily into their edges they will find that the result from their practice is harmony and strength. Vigorous postures, like warrior, fierce pose and volcano, or off-center postures, like triangle, may be challenging, but will bring the Nine to life and into their power. However, they prefer an easy going style of yoga, with a gentle pace, and encouragement, like Kripalu. They have a natural peacefulness and they will find that pranayama and meditation come easily. Yoga will also help them to better identify their own needs. Nines tend to merge so much with others that they can forget themselves. Yogic self-inquiry offers a chance for Nines to set goals about what they personally want. Mastering a challenging pose of their own choosing is a way to bring this learning into reality. As yoga teachers they can bring peace and calm to class just by being themselves. They need to recognize the awesome value of this; the world needs their calming energy.

Details for Nines

Since the Primary center – the **Gut-Instinctual** center – is what gets out of balance, focus instead on the other centers: **Heart** and **Head**. Decide to do this practice for you – just for you. Bring your heart into the practice – go ahead and make this practice all about you.

Focus on the out-of-balance Unused center: the **Gut-Instinctual**. Get into the practice and confront those edges with curiosity and passion. Be present fully. It's often uncomfortable – Breathe! Dive into a strong physical practice. Do a lot of standing postures, especially off-center postures like triangle, and challenging balancing postures.

Practice being present with a strong, deep Ujjayi breath. Breath of Fire, both Kapalaphati and Bhastrika, will energize and ground you. Nines really don't need many preliminaries in order to get into a deeply relaxed and meditative state, but doing a strong breath first will help you be more focused when you meditate.

Stay present in Savasana and in meditation, don't go to sleep. Here's a trick to staying awake in Savasana: bend the elbows and let your hands flop at the wrist. You can relax while they hang there in the air, but if you fall asleep they will fall over.

After Savasana, try this: finish with a celebration of your strength which is combined with a deep peace and harmony, by ending practice with strong Ujjayi breaths, sitting or standing in Volcano pose.

Volcano – Inhale as the hands press together and lift up; exhale as the arms open out wide and pull down. Repeat several times, feeling your power.

Meditation for Nine – Peacemakers

Holy Love is active and moves through our lives, yet also brings unshakable Peace. Visualize yourself riding colorful ribbons of love through the Universe, bringing Harmony to all and transforming all in its wake. Your very presence allows people to feel peace and connect with their True Selves. You feel connected to All that Is. Think to yourself: I exist! I am empowered.

Results: Integrated and Awake as you shift to the presence of Three.

Type Nine – Questions for Self-Inquiry:

1. What postures do I like? Why?

_____

_____

_____

_____

2. What postures do I dislike? Why?

_____

_____

_____

_____

3. Are the reasons for your liking or disliking a particular posture more physical or emotional or something else?

_____

_____

_____

_____

4. Does my self-talk during practice have a common theme?
   If so what is it?

_____

_____

_____

_____

The Spirituality of the Enneagram and Yoga

"We are spirit, in the material world."

– Sting

The symbol of the Enneagram and its sacred energy was originally introduced to the West by Gurdjieff who discovered it during his exploration of the mystery schools of the Middle East. As such, the Enneagram has much in common with the tradition of yoga, which is also an Eastern mystical path which has been integrated into our modern Western thought. By definition, mystery schools are founded on the experience of Awakening to Source, "the universal insight that human beings are spiritual presences incarnated in the material world and yet mysteriously embodying the same life and Spirit as the Creator."[33]

Identifying the ego patterns and personality habits that we usually think of as our identity is essential in the process of realizing our true identity, Divine Essence. We must explore who we think we are, and discover that this personality identity isn't actually who we are after all, before we can clearly perceive our True Self. Both the Enneagram and the discipline of Yoga are tools that help us to understand and transcend this illusion of the ego. Both systems have the same purpose. The difference, I believe, is that the Enneagram offers a psychological construct to identify the patterns of illusion, whereas yoga offers techniques and disciplines to eliminate them. Once identified, destructive patterns can be eliminated; therefore, I believe, the Enneagram and yoga work well together.

The Enneagram points to our Essential nature, from which our ego constructs a warped impersonation as an attempt to reconnect or recreate the experience of being in Source. It is an expression of our longing for our home, to reunite with the Divine. When we identify this ego fixation as it is, we are then free to identify with ourselves at a deeper level, discovering our Essential nature. We awaken our connection to Source.

Yogic philosophy is based on the mystical experience of Spirit, the Divine Self, the Atman, God, Source individuated in each of us. In the spiritual disciplines of yoga, first we study the outer self, the body and the mind, recognizing that it is all connected. By attaining physical and mental mastery, we get beyond the habitual busy identification with mind and body (maya). As we become a witness to the intrigues of the mind, we begin to experience "that which is the witness" and this leads to the universal experience of Grace, Essence, or what many yogis call Being-Awareness-Bliss (sat-chid-ananda). The Yoga Sutra defines yoga as the state of mind when one has learned to cease identification with the fluctuations of the mind. It is only then that one discovers his True Nature and experiences Bliss.[34] The Enneagram helps us to identify these fluctuations, move beyond them and thus allow us to go into the Bliss.

The challenge on the spiritual path is that we are so easily fooled. Our ego is very real and is a great trickster. I have known some very unbalanced, unhealthy "spiritual" people who are not near as self-aware as they would like to believe. The Enneagram is valuable because it shows us how our ego gets stuck in patterns, or samscaras (a Sanscrit term), that keep us from experiencing our Essence. It gives us a pattern or map of the terrain of these mind games that are so insidious we act them out unconsciously. When we become aware of these patterns though, it is like a light is turned on and the unconscious pattern becomes conscious. Then we can detach from it and the result is an experience of self-understanding and ultimately of Grace. Enlightenment is mostly a matter of getting out of our own way.

When I found the Enneagram it was profoundly awakening for me. This knowledge helped me to see the patterns that I so closely identified as the truth. Having the Four pattern, I did not think I lacked introspection, which I now recognize as really self-absorption, critical self-recrimination and ruminating. What I did lack was an understanding of my particular pattern, how it shows up and what to do about it. So my attempts at introspection alone were missing the mark and running me down. Knowing the Enneagram, I now more often identify the emotional lows for what they are and thus, their power over me is diminished. I am also more likely to recognize the emotional highs for what they are, not confusing them with any kind of spiritual mastery. My challenge is to enjoy them without becoming attached. When the emotions are quieted, the doorway to an even deeper experience is available. Equanimity is the key to my spiritual door. I can more likely catch myself before I get stuck in the hole of self-recrimination. My faith in the Divine has been strengthened and it transcends the particular mood of the moment.

The Sacred text, *Bhagavad Gita*, is a beloved story in the much longer epic Mahabharata, the tale of the ancient Indian people.[35] In this story, acting as friend and charioteer, Krishna instructs the Warrior-Leader Arjuna in the paths of yoga. Arjuna, like most of us, is facing battles and conflicts that are ethically confusing to him. The interesting thing about the *Bhagavad Gita* is that it gives different instructions for connecting to God through the three centers. These centers are Action-Gut, Devotion-Heart and Contemplation-Head. Those who identify with the Gut center, Eights, Ones and healthy Nines, would best be able to connect with the Divine through Karma Yoga, the yoga of action. Those who identify with the Heart center would be able to connect with the Devotional aspect of yoga, Bhakti, the yoga of worship. Those who identify with the Head center would connect with Jnana yoga, the yoga of contemplation. Buddhism is a part of this tradition of contemplation. Finally, the *Gita* gives respect to the joining of all three approaches in Raja Yoga, the Royal Path. The idea is that though we might feel most comfortable with one approach, in the end we'll benefit by expanding into all of them.

Though there are the three Centers and three ways to connect with the Divine, each Enneagram type has its own special core memory and relationship with that Divine connection. The Divine, for a Four, is alive and creative, the One Source from which everything emanates. This is the particular version of Divine Experience through the "four screen." The beautiful thing to me is that there are at least nine primary ways to experience Divine Essence and awaken to Source.

The Ones experience Source as Perfection, the Twos as Love, Threes as Magnificence and Beauty, Fours as Creativity, Fives as Intelligence and Wisdom, Sixes as Faithful Communion, Sevens as Bountiful Joy, Eights as Omnipresent Power, and Nines as Peace and Harmony. Like colors of a rainbow, they make up the spectrum of the Divine Experience.

Yoga Recommendations for each Type END NOTES:

30. *Awakening the Spine* by Vanda Scaravelli. A beautiful inspiring book and proves age is no real handicap to doing yoga.

31. *Yoga: The Spirit and Practice of Moving into Stillness* by Erich Schiffman. An easy and inspiring read. Lovingly explains the spiritual practice of yoga.

32. In the following meditations for each type I mention the Holy Ideas, which were taught by Oscar Ichazo and discussed by Riso-Hudson in *Understanding the Enneagram*.

33. *Wisdom of the Enneagram*, pg. 9.

34. *How to Know God: The Yoga Aphorisms of Patanjali* by Swami Prabhavananda and Christopher Isherwood. My favorite editorial of the Yoga Sutras.

35. *Bhagavad-Gita* – any version is great.

Bibliography

The Enneagram Institute: **www.enneagraminstitute.com**
Yoga Nine Ways: **www.yoganineways.com**
Phoenix Rising Yoga Therapy: **www.pryt.com**

Bhagavad-Gita – any version is great.

Beckwith, Gary L. *The Message that Comes from Everywhere*. Harmony Institute, 2001.

Brennan, Barbara Ann. *Hands of Light*. Bantam Books, New York, 1987,88.

Dass, Ram. *Be Here Now*. Lama Foundation 1971, Hanuman Foundation, Crown Publishing, New York, 1978.

Desikachar, T.K.V. *The Heart of Yoga: Developing a Personal Practice*. Inner Traditions International, 1995.

Emoto, Masaru and David A. Thayne. *The Hidden Messages in Water*. Atria Books, 2005.

Gannon, Sharon and David Life. *Jivamukti Yoga*. Ballantine Publishing, 2002.

Iyengar, B.K.S. *Light on Yoga*. Schocken Books, 1966, 1977, 1979.

Keller, Dr. Mary Helen, *Enneagram Skins*. Monastery of St. Clare, Memphis.

Kirk, Martin with Brooke Boon and Daniel DiTuro. *Hatha Yoga Illustrated: for greater strength, flexibility and focus*. Human kinetics, 2004, 2006

Moore, Thomas. *Dark Nights of the Soul*. Gotham Books, a division of Penguin Group, 2004.

Myss, Ph.D., Carolyn. *Energy Anatomy – The Science of Personal Power, Spirituality and Health*. Sounds True Audio, 1996.

Prabhavananda, Swami and Christopher Isherwood. *How to Know God: The Yoga Aphorisms of Patanjali*. Vedanta Society, 1953, 1981, 2007.

Riso, Don Richard. *Discovering your Personality Type*. Boston: Houghton Mifflin, 1992. Expanded with Russ Hudson, 1995 and 2003.
Riso, Don Richard. *Enneagram Transformations*. Boston: Houghton Mifflin, 1993.

Riso, Don Richard with Russ Hudson. *Personality Types*. Boston: Houghton Mifflin, 1987, 1996.

Riso, Don Richard, and Russ Hudson. *Understanding the Enneagram*. Boston: Houghton Mifflin, 1990, 2000.

Riso, Don Richard and Russ Hudson. *Wisdom of the Enneagram Guide to Psychological and Spiritual Growth for the nine personality types*. New York: Bantam, 1999.

Scaravelli, Vanda. *Awakening the Spine*. Harper Collins, New York, 1991.

Schiffman, Erich. *Yoga: The Spirit and Practice of Moving into Stillness*. Simon & Schuster, New York, 1996.

Stryker, Rod. *The Four Desires: Creating a Life of Purpose, Happiness, Prosperity, and Freedom*. Delacorte Press, Random House, 2011.

Swenson, David. *Ashtanga: the Practice Manual*. Ashtanga Yoga Productions, 1999-2011.

Toward the One
The Perfection of Love, Harmony and Beauty
The Only Being
United with all the Illuminated Souls
Who form the Embodiment of the Master
The Spirit of Guidance.
– **A Sufi Invocation**

May our Minds be radiated with Wisdom
May our Hearts be filled with Love
And may our Bodies be Strong and Healthy.
Namaste

Inhale, and God approaches you.
Hold the inhalation, and God remains with you.
Exhale, and you approach God.
Hold the exhalation, and surrender to God.
– **Krishnamacharya**

In gratitude I remember that You
My Divine Source, Creator, Beloved
The One who knows my heart,
are as close to me as my very breath,
and always present to guide me, support me
Teach me and Love me.
In this is victorious abundance of Life!

Om Bolo Sat Guru Bhagavan Ki, Jai!

Be Still...And Know...That I Am...God.

Biography

Debi Saraswati Lewis is an artist, musician, yogi, mystic and muse. She discovered yoga in 1983 and since then has studied many forms of yoga: Iyengar, Ashtanga, Kripalu, Power Vinyasa and Viniyoga, from many beloved teachers, and has synthesized them into what she has named Joyflow. She has taught yoga for over 20 years and is registered with the Yoga Alliance at the highest level, E-RYT500. She is the owner and director of Joyflow Yoga Studio and the principle instructor of Joyflow Yoga Teacher Training, accredited by the Yoga Alliance since 2001.Saraswati has certifications in Phoenix Rising Yoga Therapy, the Enneagram (through Riso-Hudson's Enneagram Institute), Laughter Yoga and Yoga Meets Dance. She has experience and training several forms of body/energy work: Massage, Reiki, Healing Touch and Thai Bodywork, as well as in several other forms of meditative movement: DanceMeditation, Dances of Universal Peace, and Trance Dance. Saraswati had many years of training in music (classical flute) and art. She is a initiate in the Sufi Order of the West and is fascinated with living intuitively guided by Spirit. Her book, *Yoga Nine Ways: Awaken to Source with Yoga and Enneagram*, expresses her ground-breaking ideas integrating these wisdom traditions with life changing and practical applications. She is beginning to lead Yoga Nine Ways workshops and retreats around the world. Go to her personal website: **www.YogaNineWays.com** for more information.

Notes

Notes

Notes

27700460R00072

Printed in Great Britain
by Amazon